Parents, Learning, and Whole Language Classrooms

Parents, Learning, and Whole Language Classrooms

Gerald R. Oglan
Wayne State University, Detroit, Michigan

National Council of Teachers of English
1111 W. Kenyon Road, Urbana, Illinois 61801–1096

Grateful acknowledgment is made for permission to reprint the following:
Easy/Hard Chart on page 26: From *What's Whole in Whole Language?* Copyright
©1986 by Ken Goodman: Reprinted by permission of Scholastic Canada Ltd.
The material on page 82: ©Queen's Printer for Ontario, 1994. Reproduced
with permission.
The figures on pages 55, 56, and 58–60: Reprinted by permission of
Constance Weaver: *Reading Process and Practice: From Socio-Psycholinguistics to
Whole Language. Second Edition.* (Heinemann, a division of Greenwood
Publishing Group, Portsmouth, NH, 1994).
The list on page 68: From *The Mother Tongue: English and How It Got That Way*
by Bill Bryson. Copyright ©1990. Reprinted by permission of William Morrow
and Company, Inc.

Staff Editor: Kurt Austin

Interior Design: Pat Mayer

Cover Design: Joellen Bryant

NCTE Stock Number: 34955-3050

Library of Congress Cataloging-in-Publication Data
Oglan, Gerald R., 1949–
        Parents, learning, and whole language classrooms/Gerald R. Oglan.
            p.   cm.
        Includes bibliographical references (p.   ).
        ISBN 0-8141-3495-5 (trade pbk.)
            1. Language experience approach in education—United States.
        2. Education, Elementary—Parent participation—United States.
        3. Learning.   I. National Council of Teachers of English.
        II. Title.
        LB1576.036 1997
        372.62'09773—dc21   97-33187
                                                                       CIP

To Helen, Victor, Leonard, and Eulene

Contents

Foreword

I am a whole language teacher, teacher educator, and mother. While I treasure the knowledge base I developed as a classroom teacher and as a graduate and undergraduate student at Indiana University, I must admit that my children have taught me the most. Devin is five and Colin is three and a half. Together, in five short years, they have confirmed and extended the theoretical notions regarding teaching and learning that I have spent a lifetime developing. They do so because they awaken each day to live life fully, to assume the role of genuine inquirers. As they simultaneously take in and transform their inner and physical worlds, they make complex connections to make sense. As I watch my young children carefully, I am cognizant of the fact that they will only be under my care and watchful eye for a very short while. Then I, too, will join the ranks of the millions of parents who entrust a significant portion of their children's lives to public school teachers. And so it is with reverence for my profession and hope for my own children's future that I proudly introduce this book.

Gerry Oglan is a parent too. His voice reflects the fluidity with which he unites his professional and personal lives. *Parents, Learning, and Whole Language Classrooms* will promote genuine collaboration between and among parents and teachers if readers take the message to heart and mind. David Heine helped us recognize that there are tremendous differences between cooperation and collaboration. He argued that it is only collaborative ventures that foster learning and change ("Learning

Together: A Socio-Semiotic Perspective of Learning." Dissertation. University of South Carolina, 1988). While Heine's work addressed relationships between teachers, Gerry's work illustrates the transformative nature of collaboration between parents and teachers. So often parent-teacher relationships reflect nothing more than polite cooperation. Because Gerry is a whole language teacher, he is not willing to settle for what is typical. Like most thoughtful whole language teachers, he strives for what is possible. In this case, he explores the potential of solid working relationships with parents that are built upon trust and understanding. Long ago he learned to trust himself, the children, and the process. Most recently, he has added parents to this list and in so doing has illustrated how crucial it is for us to hold our model with all learners, tall and small.

While Gerry clearly addresses the power, potential, and vulnerability of whole language in an informative way, it is the voices of the parents that come through loud and clear. Because the parents entered into a truly collaborative relationship with Gerry, their perspectives are fresh, honest, sincere, sometimes biting, sometimes fragile, but always legitimate. It is the legitimacy of parents' memories, joys, and concerns regarding their own and their children's schooling that helped Gerry understand so that he could in turn help others.

Gerry knows how stories help us shape and interpret our world. Consequently, he tells stories. In fact, as a writer he uses the same literary devices to communicate his message that he argues the brain needs to come to understand or to know. He suggests that "the brain has multiple ways of knowing" and points out that the locale memory "becomes engaged through the use of stories, metaphors, celebrations, imagery, and music" (p. 32). Gerry uses such devices to effectively capture, inform, and transform readers' notions about whole language and/or relationships with parents. He does so by showing, not simply telling. The vignettes of parent workshops and parent reflections portray the uselessness of "either-or, us and them, for or against." Instead, we find collaboration, inquiry, and learning as the driving forces in experiences that foster growth.

I recently returned from a preconference institute on inquiry at the International Reading Association. Jerry Harste ended the day by suggesting that he intended to focus on collaboration with parents next year. He argued that his experiences at the Center for Inquiry in Indianapolis, Indiana, have led him to believe that our parents will help us find our most promising next step professionally. I can't wait for him to read this book.

I love the fact that Gerry acknowledges the NCTE/IRA *Standards for the English Language Arts* and reminds the authors and readers of this very important document to remember the roots of whole language. He describes whole language as a living theory and shows how it evolves with this work.

Finally, I believe that any good book that promotes inquiry should urge readers to reflect and then take some form of social action. Having reflected on the insights woven throughout this text, I want to rethink our work with parents at the Center for Inquiry in Columbia, South Carolina. And thanks to Gerry there is a sense of urgency about this important work, the kind of discomfort that will allow us to celebrate our accomplishments while also formulating new goals for parent/teacher/child collaboration. I am confident that we will find ways to make this work our own, to go to new places together . . . tomorrow.

Heidi Mills
Professor of Elementary Education
University of South Carolina, Columbia

Acknowledgments

Steve Snyder, principal of King Edward Public School, and Hilary White, principal of Princess Anne Public School, recognized a need to provide parents with opportunities to learn about whole language. They invited me into their schools to work with parents and supported the projects through their attendance at the sessions and their willingness to discuss, share, and take some risks on their own.

Without parents, this book would not have been written. I would like to thank the parent-authors from Princess Anne Public School who contributed stories to this book: Janice Kersey, Jim Alston, Diane de Groot, Sue Lenarduzzi, and Heather Mantle. Along with these parents I would like to thank Greg Zvric and Juanita Rivait, two exceptional teachers who believe whole language classrooms support all learners, for allowing me to work with them and their children on a regular basis.

King Edward Public School will always hold a special place in my heart. As a teacher I was always supported by the parents who were right there when I needed help in my classroom. I would like to thank our writing group: Bev Marshall, Joe Perpich, Julie Harder, Debbie Dunbar, Agatha Sarafianos, and Karen Rockwell-Georgiou. I will never forget our final authors' celebration and the nervousness we felt, along with the tears we shed, as we listened to our stories.

The parents from schools in the Windsor Public School Board who attended the Parent/Volunteer Inservice sessions forced me to question my beliefs about literacy. We shared our lives, and in the process we discovered the learners within all of us.

Karen Feathers, a friend and colleague at Wayne State University, helped me understand adult literacy when she invited me to teach a course with her. Together we looked beyond what we knew about adult literacy, spending many hours discussing, sharing, and questioning our beliefs about literacy.

My friends from South Carolina have always been supportive of my work. I thank Janet Files for reading the initial drafts and encouraging me to continue, and Heidi Mills for not only writing the foreword but for being a wonderful friend and mentor.

Thanks also to Averil Elcombe, a dear friend and colleague at the Windsor Public Board of Education. Her gentle nature, fresh and honest attitude toward life, and commitment to young children made working with her a very pleasurable adventure.

This book lived through five editors at NCTE, but I owe an awful lot to Dawn Boyer. When I had given up, Dawn helped me to find my way through the words. Her expertise in developing new authors was evident, and I am thankful that I had the opportunity to work with her.

My wife Maureen has always supported me in everything that I do. She's been an editor, mentor, friend, and a loving wife for over a quarter of a century. I'm also grateful to our children, Nadia and Jarrod. Jarrod has become known at whole language conferences for his ability to outsell everyone at the memento booths, for introducing authors, and for being my traveling partner. Nadia is an individual who knows what she wants and how to get it (especially from her dad).

And finally, I thank our parents, Helen and Victor Oglan and Eulene and Leonard McGuinness, for their time, love, support, and patience as our first teachers.

Introduction
"Oh, No! They've Asked Me to Write a Story"

*I*t has been a long time since I've had to place pen to paper and compose a creative piece of writing. My writing in recent years has been limited to composing letters in the office which take on a standard format and impersonal style, and making lists of all sorts—shopping lists, vacation lists, planning-the-day lists, lists of a busy mom. The writing of stories and feelings has long since been left to the past.

Composing a story in my school years was a real chore. Writing a story on a specific subject handed down by the teacher did not always inspire my creativity. And there was always the worry of losing marks for incorrect spelling. Sometimes it seemed the worry over sentence structure, spelling, grammar, and where or where not to place your punctuation consumed my every thought and there was no room in my mind for the actual invention of the story. To this day it's not easy for me to write and let the words flow in an unedited story; I still worry about the mechanics of what I'm writing rather than letting my thoughts flow uninterrupted to the paper.

So you can imagine how upset and critical I was at the start of my daughter's school year to find the work she brought home full of spelling and grammar errors. I was greatly concerned—how will my daughter fare in high school? how will she ever get a job? what will her future be like if she can't spell and compose sentences correctly??? I was an excellent speller in school—I could memorize and spell correctly all of my weekly spelling words in grade 5.

Full of concern, I'd check Kelly's work at home and suggest that she correct the spelling and grammar. But Kelly would let me know very matter-of-factly that this was just her work copy (even though it was to be handed in), and her own spelling and grammar were fine for now.

And what about exams, the dreaded exams? I admit I used to procrastinate and cram all my studying in the night before. I'd memorize word for word my notes, panicking every second. With subjects I felt confident with I would go into the classroom, write the exam, and forget all my notes within the following hour until the night before the final set of exams, when I would do my last-minute cramming again. I would panic and sometimes freeze and stare blankly at the exam. All my studying of the term's work would leave my mind. The pressure was tremendous. The actual exam was bad enough, but how about those moments the teacher would hand out the exams with the large marks printed on the sheet, or worse yet, read out the marks?

Pressure seemed to be a big part of my school years. Speeches were horrifying. To actually stand before the class and speak turned my stomach to jelly. From the moment speeches were announced, I would panic. My speech would be memorized and I would know it perfectly the night before, but as soon as I took my place to speak, my eyes would not leave the cue cards and my heart would pound loud enough that I was sure the whole class could hear. I couldn't wait to get back to my seat and hide! Even now, when my children announce they are working on speeches, the memories of my school speeches fill my mind. It surprises me how casually my children take speeches. There is no panic, little pressure, and they almost look forward to the day they present them. Perhaps allowing children to progress at their own pace takes the pressure off and allows them to relax and absorb what they are learning.

As the weeks go by I continue to read Kelly's work, not only the work from school but also notes she writes at home. I'm beginning to notice more and more words being spelled correctly. And I begin to realize that although she could not spell many words correctly, she knew many more words than I knew at her age.

Kelly writes easily—she sits at her table and writes stories and poems on her own, not because she was forced to. She may not always finish her stories, but when she reads me her unedited story, she is as proud as can be.

One night while at an arena waiting for my son's hockey game to finish, I called home to speak to my husband. Kelly answered and let me know her dad was busy and couldn't come to the phone. I told Kelly it wasn't important and that I'd see Dad when I got home, but she was not satisfied and insisted I give her a message to write down.

It's hard for me to put aside the rigid "rules and regulations" that were taught to me as a child. But I'm learning, and as I have seen Kelly progress with her writing and reading, I find myself not being so critical of the mechanics of her work but more pleased with the content.

Diane de Groote, Parent
Princess Anne Public School
Windsor, Ontario

The purpose of this book is to step back and reconsider the role of parents in education from two key perspectives. The first is from a paradigm perspective. Schubert (1986) defines a paradigm as a conceptual lens through which learning is viewed; a paradigm can be influenced by a person's previous learning experiences or by his or her present frame of mind. *Paradigm,* a buzzword for explaining structural changes in education, has been misunderstood. This book will attempt to explain the misunderstanding by examining the educational histories of parents from an "empirical" paradigm and offer new insights for readers to consider from an "interpretive" paradigm.

The second perspective is the role that emotion plays in memory and the retention of knowledge. Our memories are capable of containing vast amounts of information. Simply talking in terms of short and long term limits our understanding of the learning environments needed to support literacy and the role that emotion plays in this process. By understanding the issues of paradigms and memory, we can attempt to explain why parents have such a difficult time accepting new models of literacy such as whole language. Such an understanding also helps explain the difficulties encountered by teachers who attempt to adopt whole language practices by mixing and matching traditional and holistic strategies.

From the moment we are born our brains are designed to search for meaning. As infants grow and develop, they use inquiry and discovery as strategies in their search for meaning. Inquiry is natural to all learners (Watson, Burke, & Harste, 1989). For parents inquiry is a way of life.

From the time children are born until they leave the protective custody of their families, their parents possess an innate desire to ask questions in order to obtain information about their children's safety, security, and well-being. As parents, my wife and I are constantly asking questions of our children (Jarrod, 14, and Nadia, 18). Parents want to know where their children are, who they are with, how their day was at school, what time the baseball game is, why children are crying, and the list goes on. Parents ask questions in order to learn more about their children. It is a natural process and it is necessary that their inquiries be heard.

Watson, Burke, and Harste (1989) cite five conditions necessary for inquiry: vulnerability, community, generation of knowledge, democracy, and reflexivity. Whole language teachers consider all five when they are teaching their students. Teachers, researchers, and learners may not seek conflict, but they have no way of avoiding it when it comes (Watson, Burke, & Harste, 1989). As educational changes bring on more inquiries from people outside of the teaching profession, educators feel vulnerable. Parents, in turn, feel vulnerable whenever their concerns about their children are not addressed, resulting in negative feelings toward the school and the teacher. Continuing to ask questions of themselves and their programs will help teachers deal with the inquiry side of vulnerability.

The school community consists of families, churches, neighborhoods, and businesses. Partnerships must take into account the role that all communities play in educating children. From an inquiry perspective, *all* members of the learning community must recognize the value collaboration plays in this process.

Inquiry generates new insights about learning. By generating questions, learning is never static but is in a constant state of flux. This state of flux leads us to new ways of thinking that John Dewey (1938) defined as "educative experiences": learning events that live on in other experiences and provide us with a sense of connectedness and meaning. Parents facilitate educative experiences in the natural settings of the home and the community—and seldom do so through direct instruction. Oral language and literacy evolve over time as parents and children transact throughout their lives.

Teachers in whole language classrooms value the knowledge children bring to a learning experience. Because whole language is a theory of voice, all children have an opportunity to contribute and be heard. Just as democracies are enriched by hearing all voices, so must whole language and the profession of teaching be enriched by your inquiring voice and those of others (Watson, Burke, & Harste, 1989).

My experiences working with parents have led me to believe that they are no different. When given an opportunity to have their voices heard and their questions answered, parents extend the range of learners. This book will offer insights for educators to consider by visiting the issues of paradigms and memory and by demonstrating the role of emotion in our learning. To appreciate parents' concerns we need to develop an understanding about what guides their thinking. We must understand what paradigm parents were educated in and, as a result, how their previous experiences with learning differ from current classroom practices about learning.

As you read this book you might find yourself saying, "That sounds like me." Can you relate to Diane's story at the beginning of the introduction? Do you remember the tests, cramming the night before, feeling completely drained of all energy, asking yourself, "Why am I learning this?", feeling insecure at times? By putting meaning to some of these emotions, you will be in a better position to understand why a certain tension now exists between parents and schools over such issues as skills, phonics, spelling, mathematics, and the whole range of subject-driven curricula and how and when they will be taught.

I would like to offer a caveat. My stance throughout this book comes from my personal learning experiences. As a learner I experienced a dramatic shift in my literacy at the time when I had completed my master's degree and decided to work on my doctorate. Up to that point I had been exposed to an empirical paradigm of education throughout my life, and I wasn't prepared to deal with the interpretive thinking of my doctoral chair. It caused me a great deal of pain over the course of four years until I realized the limitations of my empirical thinking and shifted stance to an interpretive understanding of literacy. Yetta Goodman coined the phrase "kid watching" to describe what whole language teachers do in their classrooms to help them understand how children learn. I view myself as a "learner watcher." As I observe learners of all ages, the paradigm from which they operate becomes obvious from their actions, conversations, and beliefs about literacy.

The information presented in this book is a result of working with parents and others in the school system and community. Over the course of three years I conducted three microethnographic studies involving parents from schools in the Windsor Public School Board who wanted to know more about whole language. In the first study the groups agreed to meet on a regular basis over an eight-week period. During this time we read books and articles, held literature circles and discussions on a range of issues, and wrote our own families' stories. The quotes that you will be reading are from the parents in the writing projects. The second study involved thirteen parent workshops that I conducted over a six-month period in other schools. These sessions were held in the evening and covered topics such as reading, writing, and spelling. The third study (dealt with in Chapter 5) involved a group of parents and volunteers who help classroom teachers listen to children read or help them write, edit, or revise stories. Averil Elcombe, an Early Literacy Consultant with the Windsor Public Board of Education, and I developed an inservice program that taught parents about how children develop as readers and writers and had them experience many of the strategies that whole language teachers use in their classrooms.

Parents are demanding to be more directly involved in the education of their children. Educators and parents who set boundaries and take an "either-or" position about education and the roles that all parties must play only fuel the existing fire and do little to influence change where it is needed in the classroom. In 1990 Heidi Mills, my doctoral chair, first introduced me to a strategy she called Three Pluses and a Wish. My work with parents has provided me with many pluses; my wish is that you will walk away from this book with a better understanding of why parents think and react the way they do about educational change, and that you find a little piece of yourself within and across these chapters. I hope that you use this information within your communities to work on behalf of all learners because, as Ralph Peterson (1992) has said, "community in itself is more important to learning than any method or technique."

1 The Parent Dilemma

A colleague, Greg, asked me if I would attend a parents' night at his school. He was new to this school and was implementing whole language philosophy in his grade 5 classroom. He asked me to attend the parent session because he was concerned: his new school was traditional, and the parents were not supportive of whole language. Parents were not afraid to speak out, and they felt comfortable with the traditional program that had been offered over the years. Greg knew the issue of invented spelling would inevitably come up, and since my research involved invented spelling he felt I would be in a better position to answer questions that parents would be asking.

That evening eighteen out of a possible thirty parents showed up. Greg started with an overview of his program, showed samples of students' work, and discussed whole language philosophy. Halfway through his presentation, one of the parents asked about invented spelling. Actually, this parent went a little further, declaring that the educational system was failing his son because Greg and the school did not insist on correct spelling. This complaint led to a chain reaction, with one parent after another questioning invented spelling, process writing, reading programs, and mathematics. At this point I joined in the discussion: I shared with the parents samples of my research, and we discussed their concerns. We spent an hour and a half talking about the writing samples and examining what children knew about grammar, punctuation, and spelling. At times some of the parents shouted and expressed their frustration with a system they could not understand—a system that was far different from the one they had gone through, a system that did not seem to know how to explain whole language to parents. Greg and I continued to show and explain whole language using writing samples, and we referred to the parents' experiences in school. Some parents shared stories about good and bad experiences while others maintained a return to basics. As the evening went on, the animosity and anger subsided. By the time the evening was over, the parents were not totally convinced, but many felt more comfortable learning what whole language was and what it meant for children as opposed to what they were led to believe it was not doing. One of the parents came up to us after the session and said that he felt bad about the way that he was treating his daughter at home, because one night he noticed her working on a draft of a story, saw the invented spellings, and yelled at her for all of the errors she had made. When his daughter tried to explain that the inventions were acceptable because it was a first draft, he would have no part of it. He said he was going home to apologize to her and to try harder to understand how much learning has changed since he was in school.

That week another parent sent Greg a note (see Figure 1.1) thanking him for his impromptu parents' workshop. Greg's situation is representative of situations that occur in many schools. It typifies the dilemma that exists between parents wanting to know and the changes in theories of instruction and learning, both of which have changed considerably since the parents were students (see Figure 1.2).

When parents feel caught between their learning experiences and current changes in learning theory, their reaction can take the form of a phone call to the school, teacher, or principal, an interview with the teacher, or an evening with a teacher like Greg, who was attempting to inform parents of what to expect about his program. Sometimes what results is tension, and when questions are not answered, anger can erupt, with parents turning to elected officials to help them solve their dilemmas. Why does this happen? A closer look at the paradigms and systems in which parents were educated can help us to explain why they have trouble coping with change.

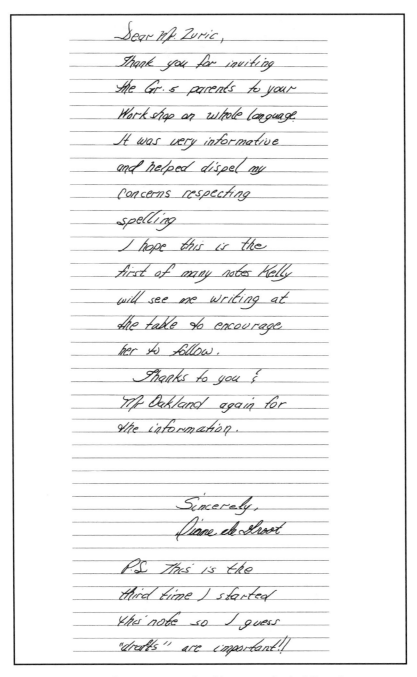

Dear Mr. Zuric,

Thank you for inviting the Gr. 5 parents to your workshop on whole language. It was very informative and helped dispel my concerns respecting spelling

I hope this is the first of many notes Kelly will see me writing at the table to encourage her to follow.

Thanks to you & Mr. Oakland again for the information.

Sincerely,
Diane de Groot

P.S. This is the third time I started this note so I guess "drafts" are important!!

Figure 1.1. Note from a parent thanking Greg for holding the parents' workshop.

Paradigms: Where Have We Been?

What is a paradigm? Lincoln and Guba (1985) define a paradigm as a systematic set of beliefs accompanied by a methodology. This chapter focuses on two paradigms that have affected education and educational change over the last century, namely, the empirical paradigm and the interpretive paradigm. The empirical paradigm represents the school system that parents and the majority of teachers were educated in, while the interpretive paradigm supports a contemporary holistic understanding of learning. The two paradigms were not intended to be mixed and matched, yet this is precisely what happens in transition, thus creating tension and uninformed media reports, and sending many whole language teachers into hiding. The conflation of paradigms is also one of the reasons why doubts hover over the issues of skills in whole language classrooms and why explanations have not informed parents enough to satisfy their inquiries and make them feel confident that their concerns are being met.

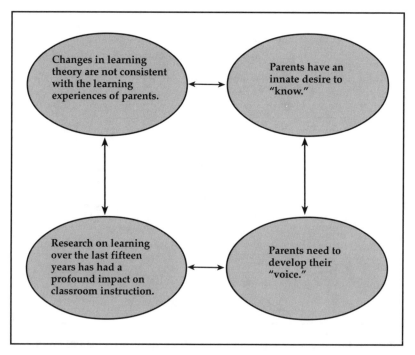

Figure 1.2. The parents' dilemma.

Let's take an issue like invented spelling. In my school district the very mention of "invented spelling" strikes terror in the hearts of whole language teachers, who say they have to develop alternative terms so as not to draw attention to their programs. When I ask parents what explanation was given to their inquiries about invented spelling, the most common response to their question was "Don't worry about it, they will outgrow it." This is the last thing that a parent who was brought up with weekly spelling dictations, spelling bees, spelling drills, and a student spelling textbook wants to hear. Teachers make these statements for a number of reasons, none of which point to an informed answer to the parent's question. Teachers who place themselves in this position cannot provide the necessary answer from a holistic perspective because they have neither accepted themselves as learners nor understood the interpretive paradigm.

Empirical Paradigm

We defined a paradigm as a set of beliefs with an accompanying methodology. The empirical paradigm has its roots in the behavioral model that originated in the late 1800s and continued through the late 1960s and early 1970s, at which time it shifted to a cognitive methodology. Figure 1.3 illustrates an empirical perspective of learning and methodology.

Belief/View	Methodology
View of language	Closed
View of context	Formal
Response to errors	Eliminate
Meaning found in	Text
Role of the learner	Passive
Motivation	Extrinsic

Figure 1.3. Empirical view of language learning.

Learning

In order to understand why parents think the way they do about education, it is important to step back and examine each one of the beliefs/views and methodologies from Figure 1.2. In doing so I present this information for the purpose of reconstructing a learner profile of parents. It is not my intention to criticize or make judgments about the empirical paradigm, but rather to use this information as a lens to view the educational history of parents and the learning implications of such a model.

Closed Systems

In a closed system, language learning is viewed as a part-to-whole method. In reading, students were required to learn sounds and letters before moving to reading words and then to reading sentences. The information was presented in a sequence, and the learner had to master the concepts in each sequence before moving on to the next step. In a subject like spelling, students were taught the same words using word lists or spellers. Letters and sounds were taught first, words were taught using the letters and sounds, and sentences took their form from the words.

Agie Sarafianos, a parent of a child at King Edward Public School, recalls her experiences with spelling:

> I remember coming home with spelling homework. Take the words from the speller, write them out ten times each, look up the words in the dictionary, and separate the words to show the proper syllabication. Is the word a noun, verb, or adjective? Now, use the word in a sentence and the trick was to come up with a sentence that no one else thought of so that when you were asked to read the sentence everyone would be impressed with your command of the language.

When meaning is the same for everyone, a closed system exists.

Formal Context

A formal context exists when the teacher imposes on the students what is to be learned, read, or written about. For example, in reading, basal readers were used exclusively. Students learned the words to a story through drill and memorization prior to reading the story. Once these words were mastered, students were expected to read stories in large groups. Students took turns reading aloud to their peers while the teacher listened for mispronounced words, immediately correcting the readers' errors and making sure they could pronounce the word before reading further. In a formal context, students were given the topics of the stories they would write about and, sometimes, the number of words they would use. Diane de Groote's story at the beginning of the Introduction highlights the issue of imposition. She states, "Composing a story in my school years was a real chore. Writing a story on a specific subject handed down by the teacher did not always inspire my creativity . . . to this day it is not easy for me to write and let the words flow in an unedited story." By imposing what students were expected to learn, teachers took the ownership of the activity out of the hands and minds of the students and placed overall control in the hands of the teachers. There was little room for individual thinking, and students were expected to "conform" to their teachers' wishes.

Response to Errors

Errors were viewed as a student's failure to learn. By concentrating on eliminating errors, teachers made accuracy the focus for all activity. Students were evaluated on the number of correct responses and graded via letters, marks, and percentages. Marks were often posted in the classroom for everyone to see. Perfection was the goal for the end product regardless of the subject, and this was mostly achieved through memorization, drill, and repetition. The focus on perfection affected students' responses to tests and exams, causing stress and anxiety, as this parent expressed:

> And what about exams, the dreaded exams? I admit I would procrastinate and cram all my studying in the night before. I'd memorize word for word my notes, panicking every second . . . . The actual exam was bad enough, but how about those moments the teacher would hand out the exams with the large marks printed on the sheet, or worse yet, read out the marks?

Meaning and Text

Meaning refers to what learners bring to a situation and how they interpret events based on prior knowledge. Meaning in an empirical paradigm was addressed through repeated exposure to the text. For instance, objects are associated with words presented by adults. Repeated associations of objects and words form a bond (Harste, Woodward, & Burke, 1984). Practice and participation through repeated drill enhanced learning when the learner was aware of the approximate success of each trial or action. The student found meaning in the text— or in many cases in how the teacher interpreted stories and word meanings—and explanations were based on the teacher's perspective, which affected such things as evaluation and assessment. The teacher relied on the information from teacher manuals to help explain meaning. As one parent commented, "The book reports and interpretations of poems always bothered me. Why should my interpretation be any more or less valid than what the teacher's manual said?" With meaning being text driven, little attention was given to individuality and prior knowledge. The authority in the classroom was the teacher and the texts and manuals he or she relied on to establish meaning.

Passive Learners

The learner's role in the empirical model is viewed as passive. Students were presented with the information to be learned, and their learning was controlled by the teacher. Quiet rooms were considered to be productive and conducive to learning:

> I remember school as being more rigid than it appears today. I always felt like the teachers were always talking at me. There was very little involvement required from the students. When we weren't being talked at, we were copying pages from the blackboard. I don't condemn the teachers of this day for this. It was the style of schooling at the time and it was expected.

Authority seemed to dominate what was done, when, by whom, and at what time. The saying that "children should be seen and not heard" was the rule of thumb:

> I remember sitting in our neat little rows following one little voice reading out loud from "Mr. Whiskers," not daring to read ahead because you might be called upon and not know where to pick up the story.

Motivation

The teacher used positive reinforcement to reward accuracy and good behavior in the classroom, a method of motivation advocated by

B. F. Skinner. In 1954 Skinner developed a number of systematic programs based on the premise that immediate reinforcement was effective in influencing learning (Shepherd & Ragan, 1982). Extrinsic motivation based on rewards and punishments reinforced the elimination of error or was used to control unacceptable behavior. Another method of motivation was grouping. Students were grouped according to their grades and their ability to compete. The "Jets" reading group was the fastest, and its members were among the first to finish their work, while the "Turtles" always needed extra time to "get caught up."

> As I think back on my early years in school I don't recall being an exceptional student. I think I was what you would call "average." I had to change schools when I was in grade 5 and didn't do well in the transition, so I failed and had to repeat the year. I remember being devastated, fearing being labeled a "dummy." It didn't do much for my self-esteem. I was only ten at the time.

Reflecting on the Empirical Paradigm

The explanations and statements made by many of the parents who participated in the writing projects provide us with a deeper understanding of their learning histories. Throughout the writing project parents identified aspects of their own learning and compared them to their children's learning experiences in whole language classrooms. Following are some key features of the empirical paradigm that were not mentioned but that are important to an understanding of the powerful influence it had on learning.

This was not a paradigm that encouraged risk taking, a fact made apparent as I worked with the parents. Many parents believe in accuracy first and had a difficult time writing drafts or expressing themselves in writing without worrying about the surface-level features of the text. Reading and sharing what they wrote was equally difficult:

> The idea was to bring parents together through the process of writing a story, discussing and editing our stories, and finally publication and celebration. This was a very scary proposition to me. Writing a story would be difficult enough but to read it aloud and discuss it with the group left me feeling very nervous.
>
> Having written a few paragraphs on an experience in high school, I realize that I have some degree of difficulty in putting my thoughts on paper. Possibly this difficulty is due to the fact that I am rarely required to write in this manner.

Conformity was expected, and the factory model of learning was present, so called because schools up to the late 1960s were modeled after industry: mass-produced materials with flawless end products; workers who were expected to perform their jobs diligently and who were expected to be members of the status quo. So ingrained is this model that it is one of the major issues facing individualized learning:

> My marks in French were always in the 90s. In grade 10 French dropped to the 70s because the teacher expected everyone's notebook to look the same. Underline here, in red, double here. I was so busy making sure that the underlining was what the teacher wanted that the confidence in what I knew faltered.

Speaking was limited to speeches and teacher-led discussions. The remainder of the time was quiet work time. Accustomed to this structure, many parents felt uncomfortable speaking in groups or with people they did not know. As I observed some of our initial meetings, people were tentative about the social aspect of learning. They needed support and reassurance that they would not be embarrassed in any way and that no question or comment would be rejected, so we initiated a process of "social construction"—something that was foreign to most parents.

> Writing a story would be difficult enough, but to read it aloud and discuss it with the group left me very nervous. However, we were a small group and "bailing out" just didn't seem right. Surprisingly, words began to flow and I actually began to enjoy writing my story. I could focus on meaning, and it was nice to know my spelling and grammar would be taken care of in the final edit.

> The characteristics of the empirical paradigm, parents' comments, and the learning experiences shared in this chapter provide us with an understanding of the parents' learning experiences. This understanding acts as a reference that allows us to examine the interpretive paradigm that supports whole language philosophy, to which we turn in the next chapter.

2 Where Are We Now? The Interpretive Paradigm

Paradigms refer to our beliefs about learning. After working with parents, I realized that part of the difficulty they were having in accepting whole language classrooms and curricula was a result of their belief systems. They were operating under a skewed belief system that used bits and pieces from the empirical paradigm to try and explain whole language. In this chapter it is necessary if not crucial to have a clear understanding of what the interpretive paradigm represents. Before we look at the interpretive paradigm, I would like you to clear your mind and keep it open. In doing so you must let go of everything you have come to know. In this case it will be "learning." Think of it as a number line (Figure 2.1) on which you are somewhere to the left or right of zero.

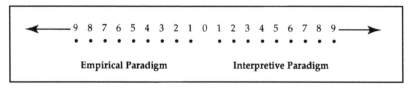

Figure 2.1. Paradigms and learning.

As a result of their learning experiences, many parents and educators operate out of an empirical perspective, or the left side of the number line. This perspective would place a person anywhere from a one to a nine, with one representing a casual interest and some concern about whole language and nine representing strong opposition to any aspect of whole language. The same could be said of the right side, which represents the interpretive paradigm. In order for parents to begin to understand the interpretive paradigm, they had to come back to zero. Coming back to the zero point places you in a new starting position.

Making the Shift

P aradigm shifts" differ from "pendulum swings." A good example of a pendulum swing occurred when open-concept education started in the 1970s. Schools were built with fewer walls, team teaching was popular, and activity-based learning became the method of delivering the curriculum. In this case the pendulum swung *within* the empirical paradigm. The physical settings and the methods of delivering curricula changed, but the other beliefs and views discussed previously were still very much in place:

- evaluation in the form of letter grades, marks, percentages
- ability groups
- basal readers
- spellers and word lists
- text-driven, page-by-page mathematics
- teacher in control

In the mid-1980s when many teachers and school districts were moving toward whole language philosophy, what occurred in many cases was another pendulum swing. This time the swing was perpetuated by a lack of understanding of whole language philosophy and theory: confusion over terminology, reading and writing pedagogy, the teacher's role in the learning process, the classroom as a community, the social nature of learning, curricular decisions, assessment and evaluation, and the role of parents in the process. What was lost in the excitement over whole language was one of the tenets of whole language, "teachers as learners." Curricula were altered to reflect a whole language philosophy, but the inservice and personal changes that require educators to question their beliefs about learning did not occur.

When parents started to question issues like invented spelling, the answers they received were not consistent with the interpretive paradigm. For example, when talking about assessment and evaluation, you cannot use terminology from the empirical paradigm. You cannot discuss a student's academic growth in terms of marks and grades. You have to return to the zero point; you need to discuss assessment and evaluation in the context of growth over time. This growth might be seen through a collection of artifacts housed in a portfolio, personal reflections in a literature response log, or a description of a mathematical concept that a student learned and expressed in a learning log. Assessment and evaluation is ongoing and is in a constant state of flux. Does this mean that tests, quizzes, and marks are not used? No, but it does mean that they are not used *exclusively* to make a determination about learning. If you are going to make the shift, accept yourself as a learner in the classroom. This means that you cannot rely only on extrinsic forms of personal motivation. Instead, do the following:

- take it upon yourself to learn and grow with your students
- read professional literature
- find out how other teachers use various strategies like the ones mentioned above
- attend professional functions and conferences
- join a support group of whole language teachers (such as TAWL—Teachers Applying Whole Language)

The Interpretive Paradigm

The interpretive paradigm emphasizes not only that learners are active participants in their learning but that the environment is crucial too—a place where learning is either enhanced or impeded (Weaver, 1988). Meaning is the central belief of this paradigm. In order to make meaning, an individual must draw upon a lifetime of knowledge, experience, and cognitive strategies in order to connect meaning to the learning experience. Thus, another key to this paradigm is accepting the prior knowledge that learners bring into the classroom. Children come to school with a vast knowledge of language patterns. What children know—their life experiences—becomes a touchstone upon which curriculum is made vital and ever alive (Harste, Woodward, & Burke, 1984). Much of this tacit knowledge is a direct result of the experiences that they have enjoyed before entering school. Parents, other family members, and peers have nurtured children's awareness about language. As oral language emerges, the role of parent or caregiver is extremely important—not as instructor, but as facilitator— through discussion, play, and demonstration (Hall, 1987). In addition, before entering school, children are surrounded by print. Most children arrive at school knowing something about written language, how it works, and what it is used for (Hall, 1987). Learning, then, is viewed as an open system (see Figure 2.2).

Learning

Identifying aspects of a whole language philosophy places us in a position to understand why parents had so many concerns about their children's learning. The questions they asked were a natural process, considering that their beliefs about learning were being challenged. The learning implications in the interpretive paradigm (see Figure 2.2) provided us with more information as to why parents were struggling with curriculum issues like spelling, reading/writing, and assessment and evaluation.

Belief/View	Methodology
View of language	Open
View of context	Authentic
Response to errors	Errors seen as miscues
Meaning found in	Prior knowledge
Role of the learner	Transactive
Motivation	Intrinsic

Figure 2.2. Interpretive view of language learning.

Open Systems

Open systems are based on a meaning model of learning that draws on previous learning experiences and the prior knowledge that an individual brings to any learning event. This means that the interpretation of text in reading and of numbers in mathematics and approaches to problem solving will differ among individuals in the class. Students may learn to solve mathematical problems using approaches and theories they have developed that are different from those used by others. Teachers create a positive environment by respecting the thinking and diversity that students bring into the classroom, and use this information as learning opportunities to teach their students about multiple ways of knowing. Teachers use questioning strategies to find the source of their students' thinking, encouraging the students' active participation. Questioning is what our brains react to as a source of motivation, as I shall explain in Chapter 3.

Authentic Context

Open systems are neither student-centered nor teacher-driven; they are learner-focused. In this context everyone in the classroom (including at times the principal, janitor, and any parent or adult who happens to enter the room) can be a voice of authority or an expert at one thing or another. When students are valued for their multiple ways of knowing, problem solving becomes a social process with students tapping the thinking potential of both their peers and the adults that surround them on a daily basis. As one parent discovered as she wrote her own family story, "People are naturally social beings. We do a lot of our learning when interacting with each other. We look to each other for assistance, answers to our questions, and solutions to our problems." Encouraging multiple ways of knowing is not restricted to written language. Meaning can be found in art, music, drama, and mathematics, among other areas. Students are invited into this system in a nonthreatening manner by taking an active role in establishing the rules and responsibility for the classroom and taking ownership for their actions.

Response to Errors

Authentic writing experiences allow students to read, write, and explore language in areas that interest them. In authentic writing experiences, errors are viewed as *miscues,* a term first used by Kenneth Goodman (1967) to describe any departure the reader makes from the actual words of the text. Goodman cited two reasons for using the term. First, he wanted to recognize that departure from the words of the text is not always problematic or something to be considered an error; and second, he wanted to emphasize how such a departure from the text indicates which language cuing system (syntax, semantics, grapho-phonemics, pragmatics) the reader is using (Weaver, 1988). Yetta Goodman (1989) viewed a child's miscues as an attempt at displaying knowledge about phonics while simultaneously using the systems of language. In constructing meaning by simultaneously using the systems of language, the reader/writer follows the text itself toward a self-correcting process. When a child writes using previous experiences, conventional spellings increase because the child is rehearsing strategies that involve words previously learned. Conventionality decreases when a child experiments with new strategies within a new context. Thus, a student's writing reflects substantial signs of growth through the in-vented spellings used. Rather than rehearsing words in isolation and being tested on memory and the ability to repeat back information, as in the traditional model, a child is supported as a participant in his or her own growth by teachers who understand that learning involves taking risks and constructing knowledge about language, not simply participating passively. Once they understand the concepts, parents view this approach to language learning as much more positive than what they had:

> As each month goes by I see more positive aspects of the whole language classroom. Following our second last session I am no longer totally concerned about spelling and grammar, but more comfortable in knowing that the process will address the issue.

Children learn about spelling as they use language, and how they write is influenced by the audiences they are writing for. The invented spelling strategies that children use and the real audiences they are writing for transact. Meaning is constructed when a child is allowed to use invented spelling when drafting stories, writing in journals or to pen pals, or writing conversation. It has been wrongly assumed that unless the markings are conventional, they are not intentional (Whitin, Mills, &

O'Keefe, 1990). Experiences are the keys to language growth which involve the learner exploring and testing in a meaningful way what he or she already knows about language. Through ongoing transactions, the environment and the learner come together to generate new experiences and to enhance the potential for language growth. A learner who plays with language makes new connections and grows.

Meaning and Text

Meaning is said to be multimodal and context dependent; that is, symbols and signs—like numbers, letters, and words—and nonverbal symbols and signs—like drawings, art forms, and mimes—have meaning potential depending on the context of the situation they are presented in and the previous experiences of the individuals using them. As one parent said,

> While my memory still finds the names Dick, Jane, and Sally familiar, it is the *Sound of Music* that is deeply ingrained today. Our teacher (who was out for half the year because of health problems) made this music come alive for us. We learned the story of the Von Trapp children and Maria and learned to sing songs, and we did a production. I don't remember the second half of the year or even who the teacher was.

We can illustrate the idea of context-dependent meaning using the number 25. When working with parents, I put this number on an overhead projector and ask them to tell me what this number means. The following are some of the answers I usually receive:

- age
- anniversary
- 5 x 5
- one-fourth of 100
- 5 squared
- 25 ones
- 2 tens and 5 ones
- 100 divided by 4
- distance
- a measurement of some kind

The meaning of the question depends on the context in which it is used. In this case the above answers represent a range of possible contexts in which the number 25 could have meaning. Harste, Woodward, and Burke (1984) highlight the idea of context-dependent meaning using the golden arches of McDonald's. In studying the language development of young children, they found that young children use symbols to establish meaning. When they saw the McDonald's sign, they exclaimed "hamburger," not reading the words but constructing meaning using the symbol. This is why pictures and visual clues are used in reading to predict meaning. The meaning potential of signs and symbols has its roots in the field of semiotics, which studies sign systems.

Transactional Learners

Whenever the learning environment and the learner come together, then a bilateral effect should occur. Dewey (1938) identified this process as a *transaction*. When students transact with oral and written language, changes in what they know about language occur. One transaction should lead to another; thus, language learning is never static but is in a constant state of flux. Children learn about sounds, letters, and their relationships through their use of language. The role of the adult in this process is to facilitate this development by asking questions, not giving answers. As shall be demonstrated in Chapter 3, by asking questions we infringe on comfort zones, but questions don't threaten: they guide students into asking and answering their own questions about language. As one parent stated after a workshop on spelling, "It taught me to be more open minded and flexible when working with my daughter . . . not give her answers but ask more questions." Vygotsky (1978) identified growth as the "zone of proximal development." That zone is the distance between a student's actual development level, as determined by independent problem solving, and the level of potential development, as determined through problem solving under adult guidance or in collaboration with more capable peers. Vygotsky viewed the growth potential of a child as a social phenomenon: "What a child can do with the assistance of others might be in some sense even more indicative of their mental development than what they can do alone" (p. 85).

Motivation

In the interpretive paradigm students take ownership of their learning. Students are made to feel valued and part of the community of learners in the classroom. As in all communities, there are expectations of its members, including the responsibility for ensuring that the learning climate is supportive and free of sarcasm and put-downs. Learning is viewed as a social process, and in that process sharing, helping others, listening, speaking, reading, and writing are ways of negotiating meaning. Risk taking is viewed not as something to fear but as a strategy to learn new ways of knowing. There is no pressure, and stress is limited. As a result, students, teachers, and adults become engaged in a process of self-discovery. This engagement can be described as something that challenges your thinking to a point that does not cause you to be bored yet does not cause you to give up. It is the relaxed state of learning that the brain requires to enhance the learning potential of all students.

Reflecting on the Interpretive Paradigm

Teachers' beliefs about how children learn have a direct influence on the classroom environment. Just as we expect our students to read, write, and expand their awareness, so must we as professionals do these things. Teachers, in particular, have a responsibility to evaluate ideas and proposals on their merits and not just passively accept them on the grounds of authority, real or presumed (Allen & Van Buren, 1971). Furthermore, we must recognize the parental dimensions of schooling and learning as central to our professional performance as teachers (Macbeth, 1989). If parents are to be viewed as partners in the education process of their children, then parents' own learning must be enhanced. How this is accomplished depends on how seriously teachers take the phrase "partnerships with parents." In the past many teachers have spent entire careers with only minimal contact with parents, and some continue to do so even now (Macbeth, 1989). In whole language classrooms, however, teachers invite parents to be actively involved.

Having established a basic understanding of the competing paradigms which teachers, parents, and students must negotiate, I would now like to turn to issues of memory, retention, and emotion. Remembering what we learn over the course of our formal schooling is influenced by emotion. The memory systems that guide our thinking and the ability to retain and recall information have been traditionally presented from an empirical perspective. Research about memory over the last ten years, however, questions traditional beliefs. Using work from the parents groups, Chapter 3 takes a closer look at these issues and their connection to the empirical and interpretive paradigms.

3 Memory, Emotion, and Learning

Have you ever wondered why we can remember certain events in our lives with great detail—events that were easy or hard to learn, or events that touched us emotionally and as a result left us with the ability to remember extraordinary details? In this chapter we will look at our memory systems and examine the role that emotion plays in our learning and our lives.

When working with parent groups, I began with two strategies to highlight emotion and its effect on learning and memory. I would like you to try the first one. Select one or both of these questions and reflect on the answer before reading on in the chapter:

1) *Where* were you when John F. Kennedy was killed and *what* were you doing at the time?

and/or

2) *Where* were you when the space shuttle Challenger exploded and *what* were you doing at the time?

I started using the second questions because the groups that I was working with were too young to recall where they were and what they were doing when JFK was killed, so I used a sample question from Michael D. Lemonick's article in *Time* magazine entitled "Glimpses of the Mind," where he used a similar approach to demonstrate the powerful role of emotion and memory.

The answers that I receive from people possess incredible detail. Was your memory of one of the two events anything like the following from a preservice teacher?

> I was in grade 8 when the Challenger exploded. Me and my girlfriend had just finished volleyball practice and we were coming back from the gymnasium. We went into our room, sat down and ate our lunch. The rest of the class came into the room and sat down. Just then the door opened and our teacher was wheeling the television into the room. When one of the students asked her why she was bringing in the television she replied, "Because the Challenger just exploded and they suspect that everyone on board was killed."

Many people's stories reflect details like the one above. I usually ask four or five people to tell their stories and then return to them and ask them questions related to subjects and content that they were taking. In most of the cases people could tell me that they were in science, English, chemistry, or biology classes when the Challenger exploded. When I asked them what they were studying and learning in these subjects at that time, they are unable to answer. They can remember the details surrounding the event but cannot remember the content of the subjects or concepts that they were studying at that time. Why? Because in light of the tragic events then occurring, the information that was being learned at the time was not considered important. Robert Sylwester (1995) believes that our emotions determine what we consider important to learn. When we are emotionally engaged, we pay more attention to learning, which in turn affects our memory and the ability to retain information. Could it be that many of the things that we are forced to learn throughout our lifetimes are not important to us? It is not always a question of importance as much as it is a question of purpose and meaning. To answer this question we need to revisit the empirical and interpretive paradigms.

Emotion in the empirical paradigm was controlled by the teacher or adult. The freedom of expression in reading, writing, speaking, and listening was teacher directed. In terms of subject matter, students were told what to read and write about. Writing topics were provided for the entire class, and whether you had any prior knowledge about the topic or not you were expected to write and read to the best of your abilities. The teacher edited, revised, and assessed the work. In the process, students learned not to think on their own but to complete tasks in order to get a passing grade. This set an early pattern and message about learning for students in elementary schools, a message that continued into high school and college. Students learned to complete work for the purpose of passing the test, completing the course, getting the credit, all leading to the ultimate goal, "graduating." Unfortunately, what was left in the wake of this approach were adults and many students who cannot recall the vast amounts of information that have been presented to them during their school years. In many cases what is easily forgotten is "subject content," and what is remembered are the memories of caring teachers who made the content bearable, friend- ships that were established, social activities, and historical moments like the death of JFK, the Challenger explosion, or more recently, the Oklahoma City bombing and the O.J. Simpson criminal trial. (Where were you when the verdict was read? Chances are you can recall the event with some detail.)

Throughout our lives the information educators have told us probably varied in importance. The reason that we do not recall or use all of it is directly related to the teacher, the program, and the environ- ment in which we were expected to learn. Some things are easy to learn, and these are things we remember the most.

Parents and Learning Experiences

I wanted to find out from parents what made learning easy or hard for them as students and as adults, so I initiated an ethnographic study using groups of parents from a variety of settings. The study examined three groups of parents and their understanding about whole language, their attitudes toward learning, and the importance of collaborative experiences on understanding. Spradley (1979) describes ethnography as the work of describing a culture. From an ethnographic perspective, my interest was guided by three questions:

1. What are parents' current perceptions about whole language after being immersed in whole language theory?
2. What influence did the parents' own learning have on their understanding of and attitude about whole language?
3. What were the features of a whole language curriculum that best supported parents' understanding of teaching and learning?

Using the three questions to guide my study, I collected data over a three-year period that involved large-group discussions, individual conferences, field notes, and audio taping. The data were collected and analyzed using the constant comparison method identified by Glasser and Strauss (1967). As categories emerged, I identified patterns. The patterns and categories were then grounded back to the literature.

The following chapters will highlight events that took place while I worked with the parent groups. In phase one of the study I worked with two parent groups for a six-week period. The Princess Anne Parents Writing Project and the King Edward Parents Writing Project consisted of parents, teachers, principals, and myself. The following is a description of the first session with each one of the groups. The purpose of the first meeting was to provide the parents with an opportunity to reflect on their own learning by identifying learning events in their lives which they found easy and hard to learn.

Parent Meeting #1

I had the participants do an activity which required them to form groups and think of things in their lives that they found either easy or hard to learn. These things could be academic or nonacademic. The groups were then asked to give reasons why they considered the subjects easy or hard to learn, after which I recorded the data (see Figure 3.1).

From this data we discussed patterns that they found consistent with learning easy things. Fun, interesting, wanted to, and ownership all became patterns characterizing the easy events. Hard learning experiences reflected issues whereby parents felt they "had to" learn information that was forced upon them. They were intimidated by certain experiences that made them feel vulnerable.

EASY	WHY?
-driving a car	-involved kinesthetic learning
-visualizing an end result	-interested in art, I see the whole setting before I paint it
-putting my thoughts to paper	-could organize my thoughts easier through the writing process
-reading	-came naturally
-learning in grade school	-involved mostly memory
-giving of oneself	-was rewarding
-clogging	-was fun
-cooking	-was fun to experiment
-spelling	-involved repetition/breakdown sounds
-talking/singing	-used communication skills
	-like people
-driving	-had a good feeling for the road
-carpentry	-learned by handling/was organized
	-enjoyed seeing things come together
-swimming	-had a natural buoyancy
-phys. ed.	-enjoyed all sports
-shopping	-was social
-mathematics	-was easy to relate to
	-the world is mathematical
	-encouraged by adults
-hockey	-was interested, had natural rhythm
	-had good eye-hand coordination
	-was fun
-auto mechanics	-worked with father
	-interested, wanted to be there

Figure 3.1. Parents' views of what makes something easy or hard to learn, and why.

HARD	WHY?
-teaching children responsibility	-involved the issue of losing or gaining control
-sewing	-faced with a mental block— getting past it
-learning written expression	-meant exposing yourself, being vulnerable
-ice skating	-had weak ankles, involved pain, was not a string skater
-riding a unicycle	-required balance
-horseback riding	-felt fear, lack of control
-crocheting	-caused frustration
-baking	-"hated" measuring, would rather cook any day
-difficulty saying "no"	-hated to disappoint anyone
-using a personal computer	-felt intimidated
	-took a lot of time
	-didn't want to
-spelling	-couldn't visualize words
	-was dyslexic
-playing piano	-felt peer pressure
	-practice time meant missing out on activities with my friends
	-was a question of cost vs. benefits
-history	-required remembering dates
-physics	-required remembering formulas
-public speaking	-feared being in front of people
-statistics	-was hard to grasp concept
	-had no use in my learning environment
	-needed the credit to pass
-overcoming bad behavior	-couldn't control or change it
-getting up in the morning	-was not a morning person
-playing an instrument	-found finger movement hard
	-did not like to practice
	-could not understand notes
	-my dad wanted me to
-parenting	-was not "fly by the seat of your pants"; takes time, patience
	-looked for things to pass on/ teach

Following this discussion I read to the groups an excerpt from Kenneth Goodman's book *What's Whole in Whole Language?* (1986), where Goodman describes language learning as being either easy or hard:

It's easy when:	**It's hard when:**
It's real and natural.	It's artificial.
It's whole.	It's broken into pieces.
It's sensible.	It's nonsense.
It's interesting.	It's dull and uninteresting.
It's relevant.	It's irrelevant to the learner.
It belongs to the learner.	It belongs to somebody else.
It's part of a real event.	It's out of context.
It has social utility.	It has no social value.
It has purpose for the learner.	It has no discernible purpose.
The learner chooses to use it.	It's imposed by someone else.
It's accessible to the learner.	It's inaccessible.
The learner has power to use it.	The learner is powerless.

Parents expressed the opinion that most of their learning was equated with the "hard" characteristics identified by Goodman. These views were also supported by the characteristics of an empirical paradigm (Chapter 1), the methods used to deliver learning, and the stories the parents wrote and told during our time together. Parents felt they were not taught to view learning as "fun." Fun was reserved for playgrounds or after-school activities. In the classroom playing games was fun, but many viewed schoolwork as hard, and if it was not hard then you were not learning anything. Parents want their children to work hard but at the same time enjoy their learning.

James P. Garvin (1987) asked over one thousand parents of ten- to fourteen-year-olds, "What would you like the middle level school to provide for your child?" I decided to ask a similar question of these parents. In his study Garvin found that the most common answer was safety, from the time the children left home until they returned at the end of the day. The answers from the parents I worked with (see Figure 3.2) focused on instilling a love of learning, enjoying school, being happy, having teachers extend their children's learning, being good citizens, and teaching their children the necessary academic skills they will need to succeed in a career.

The experiences parents found easy and hard to learn beg the question of the role emotions play in learning. If what we learn is influenced by emotion, how can we use this information to understand and enhance learning? What parents want for their children may be reflected in a whole language philosophy that is being supported by new research on the brain, particularly in the areas of emotion and memory.

Memory Systems

If the purpose of schooling is to provide individuals with information that they will need to succeed as adults, then it would seem that the time spent in formal schooling should provide experiences that enhance our memories so that we can recall the vast amount of information presented to us. But this is not the case. Many hours in formal schooling from kindergarten to high school are spent on activities that do not support the retention of knowledge. In fact, these activities may cause the memory systems to "shut down," causing us to forget what we

-experiences that create a joyful learner
-appreciation of learning
-interest in learning
-a good grasp of the basics
-respect of each other
-organizational skills
-freedom to create and express
-responsibility in a "community"
-a challenging learning environment
-enjoyable learning
-recognition for their achievement and progress
-the ability to enter high school, college, university, and the workforce and excel
-a well-rounded education—mental, physical, emotional
-tools by which she can read, write, add, subtract and think in concrete and abstract terms
-an education that will allow her to appreciate life

Figure 3.2. Parent responses to the question "What would you like the school and the school system to provide for your children?"

learn. This runs counter to what educators profess as the purpose of schooling.

Part of this counterproductivity lies in the beliefs of the empirical paradigm. These beliefs are rooted in behaviorism that supports the teaching of information from a "part to whole" approach. In the empirical paradigm, all information, regardless of its subject content, was broken down into small components. Drilling information was the common approach used. It was believed that drill work was like any discipline, and in order to get "good" at something you had to drill and practice until the task or information could be recalled without hesitation or thinking. This method was based on impulse and reaction. Sports is a popular metaphor used to reinforce the idea of drill. Athletes drill and practice every day to perform their jobs in an athletic event. In doing so they break down plays, analyze movement, and work on timing, performance, and execution in order to achieve the end result: to win. This approach may work for athletes who rely on drill and practice to perform tasks automatically in highly stressful and emotional situations, but it does not work for learners, at least in terms of their memories and retention of knowledge. Contemporary brain research says that this is not how the brain—in particular the memory systems— functions. You cannot isolate the spelling neuron and say that by drilling it on a regular basis it will improve spelling and writing; there is no such connection. Caine and Caine (1991) identified two memory systems, taxon memory and locale memory. Understanding how these two systems function and their connection to emotion and attention provide us with new insights to consider about learning, the retention of knowledge, and memory.

Taxon Memory System

Taxon memory is driven by outcomes and performance. These are achieved through behavioral objectives that state what the student will learn before the learning takes place. The objective drives the outcome in that the final measurement of learning is determined by a grade in the form of a mark, letter grade, percentage, or a pass/fail. Students in elementary schools usually have no choice in learning the material but thrive on the competitive nature of the approach. Students are required to take a certain number of courses to "pass," with less concern for mastering content than for the end result of advancing to the next level or grade. In high schools (and universities) students are told they need courses from a number of disciplines to graduate and often ask, "Do I need this course to graduate?" These external products characterize the motivating forces that drive the learning:

- taxonomies or lists (generic terms—bird, house, dog, store, etc.)
- practice and rehearsal
- extrinsic motivation
- resistance to change—transfer of knowledge does not occur easily
- items existing as stable entities and not interacting with other items stored in memory (phone numbers, driving a car, etc.)
- information void of context or meaning
- safe "routes" taken to accomplish a task; mechanical approach
- information as static

Our taxon memory stores generic forms of information in the form of common nouns. We know and identify these items by their general characteristics. We go to a *store*, a *dog* is loose in the neighborhood, *birds* are getting ready for winter, the *car* is in need of repair. The information has no purpose, meaning, or context and exists to help us identify, clarify, and communicate in a general sense. The most significant feature of the taxon system is its reliance on "routes" to accomplish a task. "Routes" refers to the manner in which we approach a task and the way we solve problems. The taxon memory likes to establish "safe" routes which allow the learner to find the easiest and safest way to solve a problem. Under pressure or when faced with stressful situations, the solution is to use the easiest way out.

To illustrate this concept, I use the story of my son, Jarrod, who came with me to Pittsburgh for an NCTE conference. Neither one of us had ever been to Pittsburgh before. We managed to find our hotel and were provided with a map and directions on how to get to the convention center, which was in the downtown area approximately 5-8 miles from our hotel. Jarrod, who prides himself on map reading, acted as the navigator and directed me along the routes suggested by the map. Not knowing the city, we did not deviate from our route and for the first two days felt comfortable traveling back and forth. Our curiosity eventually took over, however; we began to make some connections to different streets and wondered if by taking a certain turn and using an alternative route we could get to the convention center faster. We tested our hypotheses and found ourselves trapped in a maze of one-way streets in an area that was foreign to us. Under a slight amount of stress, we did what people in these situations normally do and immediately looked for a way to get us back to the familiar route we had been using. Once we found it, we were able to continue along to the convention center. The story reflects what the taxon memory system does best: it uses bits and pieces of information to maintain a safe environment and thrives on "comfort zones" when dealing with situations. Think of this in the context of the empirical paradigm.

The Taxon System and the Empirical Paradigm

Taxon memory can be applied to learning in the empirical paradigm. Children are expected to establish safe routes in their learning and approaches to problem solving. Adding, subtracting, multiplying, and dividing are done by everyone in the same way using the same steps. Students are rewarded using extrinsic motivation techniques such as stickers, stars, stamps, grades, and tests, all in the name of finding out who has memorized the presented "routes of learning." When they fail to remember the exact sequence (like Jarrod and I did when we ventured away from our route), they are brought back to the comfort and safeness of task by reviewing the correct procedures. Over time students find it very uncomfortable to "transfer knowledge" learned in one context to another. The taxon memory system resists change. When confronted with situations that involve change, it becomes "agitated" and resorts to safety.

This could be why so many people are resistant to change and reluctant to make a paradigm shift. Throughout their lives they have been taught that the focus of all learning relates to comfort and safety. Is it any wonder that the interpretive paradigm which supports holistic learning is perceived as such a threat to the safety and learned behaviors of the empirical paradigm? Yet, more research is discovering that the brain works and learns best in conditions cited in the interpretive paradigm and the development of the locale memory system.

Locale Memory System

The locale memory system uses process and discovery as a means to learning. Anything learned remains in a state of flux. As a result, when it is presented with new information the system searches for meaning and tries to relate the new information to what presently exists. It thrives on anomalies, using inquiry to solve the problems presented by the new information. Everything that the locale system does has purpose and meaning and includes the following characteristics:

- is meaning-oriented, capacity is unlimited
- has memories existing in relationships and forming records of life events
- "maps" schemas that are constantly updated though experiences are recorded and developed
- is motivated by novelty, curiosity, and expectations
- is engaged through stories, metaphors, celebrations, imagery, music
- relies on "natural" memory of events
- involves emotion
- responds negatively to threat, "downshifts" to the Taxon System

The locale system records entire events as they happen. These records or "maps" exist because they involve emotion. As a result recalling the events and the details surrounding them are common (think of the example of the Challenger, JFK, etc.). When events are recalled, they can be updated as new information is presented, which in turn challenges or causes us to rethink what we know. Cognitive psychologists define these maps and the updating of information as "schemas." Locale memory thrives on curiosity and, when given ownership to explore the nature of the curiosity, relies on prior knowledge and experience. Students are motivated by the intrinsic desire to "know" and to "find out." Probably the most significant aspect of this system is emotion. Robert Sylwester (1995) states, "Emotion is very important to the educative process because it drives attention, which drives learning and memory" (p. 72). This system accepts discomfort as a way to learn. As Jarrod and I looked for new connections to find our way around Pittsburgh, we moved outside of our comfort zones by attempting to discover new routes. We were driven by our curiosity and in doing so we were updating old information with our new discoveries. We were in control and had ownership of what we were doing. We felt there was no real threat or danger in our risk taking. However, the locale system does not respond under threat, anxiety, or stress. When these conditions exist, the locale system "downshifts." When this happens it looks to the taxon system for "safe" routes or an automatic response. Think of yourself. Can you remember a time when you had to resort to using safe routes? It may have been traveling on a vacation. You tried to save time by taking another highway or shortcut, only to find yourself lost, so you returned to the major interstate you left to continue on your way. Remember substitute teachers when you were in school? Why were they so hard to get along with? Could it have been that in the absence of your regular teacher the safeness of daily routines and schedules suddenly changed and the new teacher presented a sense of threat? In doing so you probably recall yourself or several of your classmates reminding the substitute, "Our teacher does not do reading that way."

When students feel they are in control of their learning; have some ownership; use interest, curiosity, discovery, and process; and are encouraged by a guiding adult who asks questions, poses new information, and uses inquiry, they access the natural memory of the locale system. When this happens the chances increase that students will retain what they have learned. Understanding that the brain has multiple ways of knowing supports the development of the locale memory since it becomes engaged through the use of stories, metaphors, celebrations, imagery, and music as ways to express knowledge.

The Locale System and the Interpretive Paradigm

The relationship between the locale memory system and the interpretive paradigm is apparent in whole language classrooms. Parents experienced this relationship in their own learning when they completed the easy/hard activity. Those activities that were easy to learn were fun, had personal interest, and involved emotion. Brain research has implications for the classroom. Educators can no longer fail to consider what conditions are needed to best support learning. Caine and Caine's (1991) research on memory suggests that:

> [t]he learning environment needs to provide stability and familiarities; this is part of the function of routine class behaviors and procedures. At the same time provision must be made to satisfy our curiosity and hunger for novelty, discovery, and challenge. Lessons need to be generally exciting and meaningful and offer students an abundance of choices. The more positively lifelike such learning, the better. (p. 81)
>
> For teaching to be really effective, a learner must be able to create meaningful and personally relevant patterns. This type of teaching is most clearly recognized by those advocating a whole language approach to reading. (p. 82)

Caine and Caine's message about how the brain best functions highlights similarities to whole language classrooms. Words like *choice, curiosity, meaningful, discovery,* and *lifelike* (authentic or real situations) are embedded within a whole language philosophy.

Although the taxon and locale memory systems have been separated for explanatory purposes here, they actually support one another and interact on a regular basis. The natural tendency for educators when discussing the two systems, however, is to relate them to "pendulum swings." In doing so they establish an "either/or" situation when dealing with the two systems. This has placed both change and innovative teachers at risk. Pendulum swings do not happen within paradigms, despite what many teachers would like to believe. The shift from the empirical paradigm to the interpretive occurs when teachers change— when they question their personal beliefs about learning, take risks, and view themselves as learning. To characterize learning as either taxon-driven or locale-driven is missing the point and is destructive. Balance is crucial to understanding how *both* memory systems function and support learning. The two systems interact in various ways, including the following:

- locale system registers a "continuous" story of life experiences
- taxon system houses "parts" out of which stories are constructed
- locale system registers "entire" events at one time
- locale system recalls relevant information from the taxon system when needed

New information should always be embedded in meaningful experiences. Our schemas are updated with information when we are confronted by an experience that causes our brains to revisit the schema for the information it has about a topic, subject, or experience. The taxon system houses vast amounts of data. Most of the data consists of meaningless bits of isolated facts. What gives these facts meaning? Context. For instance, when I work with parents, in order to illustrate this point I use the example of the number 25 mentioned in Chapter 2. Showing it to the parents on the overhead projector, I received the following responses:

- age
- anniversary
- 5 x 5
- one-fourth of 100
- 5 squared

- 25 ones
- 2 tens and 5 ones
- 100 divided by 4
- distance
- a measurement of some kind

The answers reflected in the above list represent data similar to data found in the taxon system. There appears to be a number of uses for the number 25, but they are void of meaning. What gives isolated facts their meaning is *context*. Whenever we are presented with a learning situation, we use what we know about the topic based on our prior knowledge and experiences. If there is a strong emotional bond, then recalling the context will be easy. If we need to use the data from the taxon system, the brain performs a function known as "indexing." Indexing occurs when the brain scans the taxon memory looking for data that can support the context in question. Think of invented spelling. When young children write, their spelling reflects what they know about sounds, letters, and their relationships. When they are required to spell a word while writing, they use what they know about the sounds and letters to spell. Their taxon system indexes the available data and provides this data to the locale system to perform the function of spelling. This is true of all learning situations that use process, discovery, personal interests, and choice. When these conditions exist, the individual is willing to take risks, but the brain is allowed to relax. If accuracy is the focus, however, downshifting may occur, and for many children this means using "safe" language or words they know how to spell when writing. Using context or whole situation engages the locale system, which in turn draws upon the taxon system.

The Role of Memory in Learning

For years education has approached learning from the taxon system, using drill, teaching isolated facts, viewing the learner as passive, and reinforcing learning through rewards and punishments. The interpretive paradigm, whole language, and recent research on the brain support a natural approach to learning. However, the dilemma that we are talking about in this book is the conflict between the dominating empirical paradigm that has controlled learning and educated the majority of adults for almost one hundred years and the interpretive paradigm which challenges existing beliefs. Historically, the dominance of the empirical paradigm can be traced back to the "factory model" of schooling. During the industrial revolution, schools in the United States were built and organized like factories. The older schools even looked like factories from the outside, and on the inside they resembled a plant with small departments where people worked under a boss, foreman, or supervisor. Students were told what to do, when to do it, and how to do it. Bells signaled when to stop and start working. Classrooms resembled assembly lines: everyone did the same thing at the same time under the watchful eyes of the teachers. Every move was checked for accuracy and conformity, and any defects had to be eliminated. Producing a good, clean product was the goal, and failure to do so resulted in a loss of productivity.

Unfortunately, factory-model thinking still exists, and new paradigms that support the information age are not easily accepted. Many people have difficulty letting go of the power and control equated with the factory model. When a paradigm shift occurs, the same rules are no longer effective, and trying to "make them fit" is not consistent with "making the shift." The shift occurs when people question their existing beliefs about learning, view themselves as learners, and work collaboratively in addressing educational change. Until that happens the teacher/parent-digm dilemma will continue to pose limitations on learning.

4 Pluses and Wishes: Developing Voices

In phase two of the study, I met in the evenings with thirteen parent groups over a twelve-week period. I was invited by principals to discuss invented spelling and reading/writing from a whole language perspective. Following each of my sessions with parents, I asked them to complete an evaluation called "Three Pluses and a Wish" (see Figure 4.1), a strategy I learned from Heidi Mills at the University of South Carolina. Parents were asked to write three things they liked about the session and one thing they would wish for. Initially, I used the parents' responses to help guide our discussions whenever we met, and I noticed patterns forming from their responses. The patterns in the pluses generally reflected what parents liked about their child's school, teacher, or classroom; the wishes expressed concerns about the educational system in general. Once patterns were identified, categories emerged. The categories were then connected to broader issues: learning, memory, emotion, and research done in whole language settings.

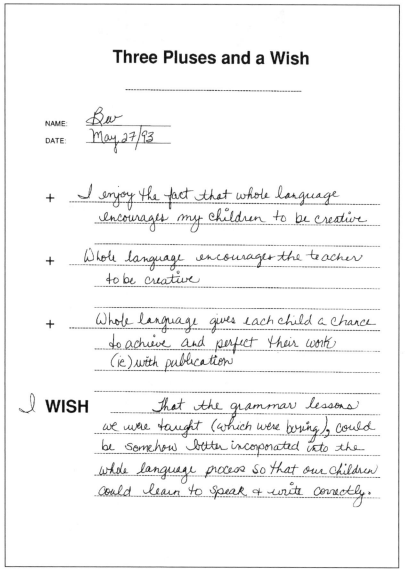

Three Pluses and a Wish

NAME: Bev

DATE: May 27/93

+ I enjoy the fact that whole language encourages my children to be creative

+ Whole language encourages the teacher to be creative

+ Whole language gives each child a chance to achieve and perfect their work (ie) with publication

I **WISH** That the grammar lessons we were taught (which were boring), could be somehow better incorporated into the whole language process so that our children could learn to speak & write correctly.

Figure 4.1. Parents' evaluation: Three pluses and a wish.

Pluses: What Parents Like

Pluses supported the paradigm shift parents made while they engaged in experiences throughout the time we spent together. Pluses reflected the connections they made about learning as a result of these experiences. Making connections, not corrections, is a belief supported by whole language teachers. The pluses parents identified about whole language were a reflection of their own learning within the context of the interpretive paradigm. This demonstrates how parents as learners were coming to understand what whole language is, as opposed to what it is not. The response patterns within the pluses underscore theoretical constructs of whole language philosophy and researchers (Peterson, 1992; Harste, Short, & Burke 1988; K. Goodman, 1986; Smith, 1989; Watson, Burke, & Harste 1989; Shannon, 1993; Newman & Church, 1990). In analyzing the pluses between the parent responses and whole language theory, correlations between theory and practice emerged. Communities of Learners, Risk Taking, Choice and Ownership, Learning as a Social Phenomenon, the Authoring Cycle, and Theory as Practice all represent philosophical beliefs of whole language researchers. The parents' comments (found at the beginning of each section) support the connections they made over the twelve weeks we spent together, and the explanations make connections to the literature review and positions advocated by whole language research.

Communities of Learners

Whole language has encouraged teachers, parents, and children to view students as a whole person—if a child is weak in one area of study, look for areas of strength and talent in other areas. Children and adults need to feel they can succeed in various aspects of their work.

As a parent I am encouraged to become involved and offer input so that parents and school share in the responsibility of education.

Ralph Peterson (1992) believes that learning is strengthened when classrooms are viewed as communities—everyone is smarter, more ambitious, and productive. Parents are openly accepted into whole language classrooms because they are a part of the learning community. They bring into the learning environment different ways of knowing. Through their life experiences, their ways of knowing become sources of knowledge to be shared with children.

Risk Taking

Whole language seems to give students inner confidence that was missing in my generation. Many students are more willing to take risks (offer opinions, alternative solutions). We sat and looked at our shoes!

I like the concept of the child as a voice to be heard and respected.

I agree that it is important for the kids to be independent thinkers as opposed to dependent thinkers.

The confidence and self-assurance that groups have out of feeling heard and free to express themselves is a definite asset in a competitive world.

I enjoy the fact that whole language encourages my children to be creative.

When children are encouraged to take risks, they have to predict and generate hypotheses about language, testing their own existing hypotheses in order to generate new patterns. Through risk taking, growth occurs over time through the functional use of language. The above observations by parents about their children's learning identify confidence, voices being heard, independent thinking, self-assurance, and active involvement in their learning; all support risk taking. The role risk plays in literacy needs to be supported, facilitated, and reflected socially in the supportive environments we create for literacy learning (Harste, Woodward, & Burke, 1984).

Choice and Ownership

Permission (even encouragement) to read books of her choice.

Subjects of interest rather than prescribed materials at a specific "level."

My children enjoy their education because it is relevant to them and their lives. Grade 1 news comes from the children, and they learn to read and write about themselves and their classmates.

Choice goes beyond reading and writing. Choice is an integral part of the language process (Harste, Woodward, & Burke, 1984). By providing children with choice we give them the opportunity to ask questions and make decisions rather than copy answers. Choice and decision making support ownership. Ownership makes learning easy when it belongs to the learner (Goodman, 1986). When children have a feeling of ownership of the tasks they engage in, teachers and parents find that their relationships with children change (Wells, 1985). This could account for the changes parents expressed in their wishes.

Learning as a Social Phenomenon

I love the enthusiasm/confidence that my daughter has when it comes to her school work.

I like the idea of my daughter's involvement with her school life experiences.

I like the idea of working in groups, sharing ideas and thoughts.

Whole language encourages co-operative learning, talking, sharing—hands-on learning is more effective, especially in the sciences.

"Individuals become literate, not from the formal instruction they receive, but from what they read, and who they read and write with" (Smith, 1989, p. 355). No one can learn in isolation. Yet many of our parents came through paradigms that believed children should be seen and not heard, and that students were passive recipients of their knowledge. Children need experiences that will allow them to discuss, share, disagree, and compare results within their learning communities. "It has been shown that groups of children can work successfully through discussion to solve problems, to explore alternative possible explanations, and to make a discriminatory response to literature. Interestingly, all these researchers noted that pupils worked more effectively when their teachers were not present" (Wells, 1986, p.189).

Authoring Cycle

Writing stories—editing and publishing (my son has been doing a lot of this in his grade 2 class).

I like the prospect of my children and other children in school acquiring the high degree of confidence in communicating and cooperating and problem solving in a group setting as such skills better prepare one for the world of employment.

Whole language gives each child a chance to achieve and perfect their work (i.e., with publication).

I like the work produced to date by children in whole language when there is little hesitation in transposing thought onto paper in an extemporaneous fashion without fear of grammar or spelling errors.

Assignments that include a lot of writing.

The authoring cycle was first developed by Harste, Woodward, and Burke (1984). In recognizing that children come to school knowing a great deal about language based on their previous experiences with print, the authoring cycle acts as a curricular framework in the classroom. Through authoring, parents see the valuable role meaning plays in writing. Once meaning is valued, surface-level features of language such as spelling, punctuation, and grammar take on new perspectives. When parents are asked to write their own stories, they come to value how difficult it is to write everything accurately at the point of utterance. Many adults were turned off from writing because more attention was given to spelling, grammar, and punctuation than to developing ideas. By drafting, revising, editing, and publishing their stories, parents made connections about surface-level features of text that they had been led to believe were not being addressed in whole language classrooms.

Theory as Practice

I like the prospect of whole language theory in practice when educators may have a chance to voluntarily change by virtue of the very process.

Whole language looks to be a practical and friendly system.

Whole language is implementing new learning knowledge, not just leaning on the possibility of outdated old systems.

Whole language encourages teachers to be creative.

Whole language is a living theory. It is living because it is generative. It is living because it is both exhaustive and full of energy. Kenneth Goodman (1986) stated that whole language is a theory of language and a theory of learning. Together, these two theories have revolutionized the profession's thinking about language learning and how it can best be supported in classrooms (Watson, Burke, & Harste, 1989). I often explain to parents that whole language is a theory that is constantly questioning itself about learning. Because we question what we know about learning, we question ourselves and the curriculum we use in our classrooms. Whole language will never stagnate. It provides a built-in self-correction device for the theory itself and for the teaching profession as a whole (Watson, Burke, & Harste, 1989).

Parent pluses reflect classroom practices. What can we say about classrooms that leave parents with these thoughts? We see classrooms that support the social nature of learning, encourage risk-taking, and provide autonomy for the learners; we see trusting environments and classrooms that view learning as a lifelong process.

Wishes: Questions and Concerns

I followed the same format with the parent wishes, looking for patterns in the wishes and connecting them to current issues from the literature and interest groups within whole language.

Developing Voices in Education

I wish I were comfortable in the knowledge that the teachers themselves were competent to deliver the "whole language programs" in a consistent fashion. However I feel from what I've heard that the program is still experimental. That teachers are learning to teach it haphazardly and in that some learning on the part of my child will be lost. My biggest wish, "the absolute best from my child." Thank you for the opportunity to express this.

When parents view learning as experimental, one of their initial concerns is with teachers. Parents want to know that teachers are consistent in their understanding about whole language and how it is being implemented in the classroom. From my experiences working with teachers, I have found this to be one of the biggest challenges facing schools, teachers, and parents. When whole language is questioned, especially by parents, most educators lack the ability to articulate to the public what whole language theory and philosophy is and how it differs from traditional programs. The answers parents get are usually linked to extraneous sources that are somehow viewed as being authorities. These extraneous sources act as "covers" for educators who are pressured by the public. Educators redirect inquiry from parents and cover them with answers that make it appear that the teacher or principal is following district, provincial, or state policy. Over time parents become confused over conflicting answers from misinformed sources. This misinformation involves the transmission and interpretation of whole language theory and philosophy by teachers, principals, and other parents with a limited knowledge base. In working with parents I have found that initially they need time to express and discuss their concerns about whole language with teachers who understand the theory. Since whole language is a theory of voice, parents' voices must be heard and valued as part of the learning community. Once they have had an opportunity to be heard, they become willing to support programs that are meeting the needs of their children and themselves. In allowing parents to be a part of this process, we are taking action to develop their democratic voices. When developing democratic voices, teachers, students, and parents place their experiences at the center of the curriculum and ask, "How do we wish to live together?" (Shannon, 1993). The following "wish" demonstrates the confusion parents are experiencing as evidenced by the statements made about whole language, high school, streaming (tracking), higher education, and teacher inservice:

> Whole language is only used in the elementary system. How will the student adjust to standard teaching methods in secondary school? Is de-streaming not the old method where all students were taught the same courses according to programs (academic, business, technical)? Will slow learners not fall through the cracks and advanced learners be bored? The current secondary system (streaming advanced, general, and basic levels) seem to better serve the whole language concept. But how can you stress this to high school teachers with twenty years seniority? Also, if there is no structured evaluation system how will students qualify for scholarships? Thus leading to college and university. Will professors with classes of 300+ in their lecture halls take the time to change their methods in order to accommodate whole language students? I suppose my questions will be answered after my child graduates. Hopefully he is not the school system's guinea pig.

This wish represents some of the issues that school systems must begin to deal with. Are these not all valid questions and concerns? Who is responsible for answering these questions? Parents today are not easily convinced by jargon and rhetoric—and with good reason! What they want for their children are teachers who know what they are doing, why they are doing it, and how they are dealing with the changes in their own learning and classrooms based on current learning theory. When parents are left to speculate on their child's educational future, they need answers from informed sources to reassure them that the risk they are taking will benefit their child's literacy in the long run.

Learning as a Lifelong Process

My wish is that my children will maintain a lifelong love of learning and the knowledge that learning doesn't stop when schooling ends.

My wish is that my children will do their best and will enjoy learning and going to school later in life as they do now.

I wish to be more aware on how to be a more productive parent/teacher.

I wish my older daughter had the opportunities whole language offers students and that I could eloquently advocate for whole language.

The NCTE/IRA standards document (1996) states that by the year 2020 citizens will need powerful literacy abilities, abilities that have so far only been achieved by a small percentage of the population. Schools need to start preparing students for a society and a workforce that will require multiple literacies. Graduating students will have to be active, critical users not only of print and spoken language but also of the visual language of film, television, commercial and political advertising, and photography. Employers will be looking for students who possess academic skills, personal management skills, and teamwork skills, as well as students who can:

- Create visual texts such as illustrations, charts, and electronic displays
- Read and write effectively in the languages in which business is conducted
- Understand and solve problems involving mathematics, and use the results

- Use current technology, instruments, and tools effectively
- Think critically and act logically to evaluate situations, solve problems, and make decisions

This last entry indicates that employers want individuals who value learning as a lifelong process. To accomplish this, students educated in an interpretive paradigm will have the ability to accept change as part of a lifelong process.

Myths about Whole Language

I wish that the grammar lessons we were taught (which were boring) could be somehow better incorporated into the whole language process so that our children could speak and write correctly.

I wish that the mechanics of grammar will be included and mastered by students in order to alleviate concerns of those who criticize the whole language theory as it evolves and becomes more utilized.

Spelling, punctuation, and grammar are important because they help the writer to make meaning clearer for readers (Newman & Church, 1990). To highlight these systems through separate lessons would render the experience void of meaning. Learning about language involves individuals exploring the systems of language. Semantics, syntax, and graphophonemics are constantly at work as children test what they know about these systems in classrooms that support risk taking. Meaning communicated through the use of personal knowledge in spelling, punctuation, and grammar is always changing as children talk, share, write, read, measure, and communicate on a variety of topics and interests.

Reflections

The pluses and wishes expressed by parents provide us with new insights to consider. Parents have an innate desire to "know," and when their questions and inquiries are not answered they become concerned. It is not a question of pleasing everyone who walks into the principal's office with a complaint. What it *does* involve is a changing attitude toward parents. Parents are becoming more visible in schools and through legislation are being given more say in the operation of schools. What parents need is information about programs and how they are taught. Holistic curricula are very different from the subjects that parents took in elementary school. They need time to discuss these issues with school administration and staff. Thus, educators have an obligation to explain and be able to articulate their programs and curricula to parents. This effort should go beyond the traditional open house and report card interviews. It involves a paradigm shift in thinking to different approaches in dealing with parents. The next chapter will highlight some of the programs that schools have used to include parents as part of the learning community. When we view parents as learners in this process and not merely as recipients of information, we alleviate stress, anxiety, and tension and replace them with collaboration, inquiry, and learning.

5 Parents as Learners

With great trepidation together we came
To explore the new beast—Whole language its name.

Our fearless leader, Dr. Oglan, guided us through
The process of writing—it wasn't so new!

We'd write and rewrite, discuss and then edit
Some laughed and some cried through each story as we read it.

Over the mountain each person did ride
Realizing how easy it was when they reached the other side.

There's really no mystery to this beast—it's a big mush
Once you face it head on then you ask, "What's all the fuss?"

We really enjoyed being part of the game
Hope you'll come back soon and do more of the same.

From your parent partners in education
King Edward Home and School

This poem demonstrates how parents came to understand their own learning. Was it easy? No! The parent groups I worked with at times expressed anger and frustration. They moved me to question my beliefs about learning more than any teacher group I had ever faced. Was it worth it? You bet! Once they had an opportunity to have their questions answered and their stories heard, barriers came down and learning took place. When dealing with parents, teachers must become listeners before they can actively engage adult learners in a literate environment (Kroeker & Henrichs, 1993).

The burden of the parent/paradigm dilemma should not be viewed as one-sided. Rather, ownership of the dilemma also rests with educators, who must think of parents as an extension of the learning community. In working with parents four questions guided our inquiry:

1. What are parents' perceptions about whole language and how did these change over time when they were immersed in whole language theory?
2. What were the features of a whole language curriculum that best supports parents' understanding of teaching and learning?
3. What influences did the parents' own learning have on their understanding and attitudes about whole language?
4. How can we demonstrate, not defend, whole language theory?

Whole language teachers question themselves about teaching, learning, curriculum, and parents. One question we must ask ourselves is, "How can we best support parents in the same way that we support students?" A whole language model is most promising because it is consistent with what we know about the learning process. Because whole language teachers share the same beliefs about learning, their classrooms may reflect the same philosophy but differ in curricular frameworks. That is why whole language classrooms often differ from traditional settings. In whole language classrooms, children read and write for real audiences. Literature study groups, literature circles, authors' circles, written conversations, personal journals, and pen pals represent a sample of potential curricular experiences. Students are encouraged to use their questions as invitations. From an inquiry perspective these invitations shape and develop the curricular framework for students. At the heart of all of these activities is a consistent theory and belief about how children learn in whole language classrooms.

When parents are encouraged to use their questions as invitations to learn more about the students they are assigned to work with, they shape and develop a lens from which to view learning. The inquiry approach involves parents revisiting their own educational histories in a supportive and collaborative environment. This results in parents feeling good about themselves, their children, the school, and the classroom.

In order to understand the impact parents have on learning, consider the following. Macbeth (1989) reported that in the United Kingdom, from the time a child is born to sixteen years of age, less than 15 percent of a child's waking life is spent in school. Murphy (1993) stated that the time spent in schools by American children based on a school year of 180 days was 9 percent. In Ontario, Canada, based on a school year of 194 days, children spend approximately 13 percent of their time in school.

These figures imply that approximately 85–91 percent of a child's first sixteen years are spent with parents, caregivers, childcare workers, or under the supervision of an adult. As school reform initiatives evolve, we must pay more attention to that other educational institution: the home (Bell, 1993). The "home curriculum" must work in a partnership with the school curriculum. This happens when schools recognize the valuable information parents can provide classroom teachers about the development of their children.

Schools need to take the initiative by providing opportunities for parents to engage in their own learning. This implies breaking away from the traditional methods of communication between home and school to more of an active involvement. A good way to get to know people is to listen to the questions they ask (Watson, Burke, & Harste, 1989). When parents sense that their questions are respected, they are more willing to verbalize and take further risks in their own learning.

Phase three of the study involved ninety-three parents who acted as volunteers in various schools. I worked with Averil Elcombe, an early literacy consultant for the Windsor Public Board of Education. We met with these groups over a three-month period. Consider some of the questions parents asked about spelling, reading, and writing:

Spelling

- At what stage in a child's reading/writing development is it okay to point out spelling errors and have him or her correct those mistakes without turning the child off writing?
- When should a parent insist that correct spelling is necessary?
- Will a child learn how to spell from copying from a book or from just reading?
- Why does it seem like phonics is not stressed as much in education today?
- Do you have any fun ways to encourage spelling at home, so that it does not seem like "homework?"
- How do we meld phonics and whole language if we believe in both?
- When mom can't spell at all well, what can she do to help her children be good spellers?
- At what age (or grade level) should children have mastered the perfections of spelling and punctuation?
- Am I wrong to go through spelling after my child has written and after I have praised her effort?

Writing

- I have a child (grade 6) who cannot write a story. How can I help?
- Journal writing is important. But when a child cannot read it back to the parent, why do teachers insist that it will come and wait until the magic testing in grade 3?
- How do you encourage original thought in writing?
- What techniques should be used in "editing" creative writing?
- How could we help a child when he or she understands the story but has a hard time putting it down in writing?
- How do we teach children when to stop and start writing paragraphs?
- When should we start teaching cursive handwriting?
- How do you encourage a child who is advanced orally but resists writing down ideas?

Reading

- At the age of seven is it okay for a child to want to read constantly from the time she gets home practically to the time she goes to bed?

- How do you get a child that has been pushed through the system to read? How do parents get help?
- What makes young children very interested in reading (even teaching themselves to read already) yet not at all interested in writing? Aren't the two media tied together?
- When is it okay to correct a child when they are reading?
- What is the best method to teach a child (age of four or five) to read?
- How do I get my son to understand what he has read?
- Can you give us more information on how to help grades 2 and 3 with reading?
- If I read aloud to my kids, should I have them read aloud to me?

Answers to these questions do not come easily. Why so many questions? I have three possible hypotheses. First, parents are starting to make a paradigm shift, and their questions should be viewed as invitations for educators to respond to, somewhat like the "teachable moment" that Diane Stephens (1990) talks about. However, in order to do this, educators need to feel comfortable with their own knowledge. This leads to a possible second answer: the source of the questions. Parents have questions because their inquiries at the school level have not been addressed, which has led to a dissatisfied attitude and frustration among parents. Much of the source of this frustration has been directed at whole language. But whole language should not be expected to shoulder the blame for the inability of teachers and educators to field the questions. The questions posed by the parents support a third possible hypothesis: the information flow from teacher/school to parents/home has not been consistent with the intended philosophy and theory of whole language. I suspect if it had, many of these questions would not be appearing in this book.

The strategies described in this book are similar to what whole language teachers use with their students across all grade levels. Good curriculum planning involves capitalizing on the interests of the learners themselves. From this perspective there is no such phenomenon as disadvantaged learners (Whitin, Mills, & O'Keefe, 1990). This perspective must be used in support of parents.

Parents and Learning: Facilitating the Shift

From the perspective of whole language, teaching is the theory of voice. Just as democracies are enriched by hearing all voices, so whole language and the profession of teaching will be enriched by your inquiring voice, and those of others. There's no need to apologize for where you are in the whole language scheme of things. There are no prior qualifications for accepting our invitation except that you bring an inquiring mind willing to be used. No question will be too small, no concern too trivial. Nor do we need to back off because you see yourself as "humanist," "intuitive," or "artsy." Some (perhaps all) of the best thinkers in education have been just that. (Watson, Burke, & Harste, 1989)

In light of the changing role of parents in schools, we initiated a program for people who volunteer in our schools on a regular basis. The majority of people we dealt with were parents who listened to students read or worked with small groups on writing. We decided that in order for parents to be more effective in their work, they needed some kind of inservice on reading and writing, so we developed the Parents/Volunteer Inservice Program. We sent letters to school principals explaining the purpose of the program and asked them to identify parents/volunteers who were working in their schools with students in the areas of reading and writing. One stipulation was that anyone recommended for the program had to commit to all three inservice sessions that would run from 9:00 a.m. to 11:30 a.m. over a three-week period. We received fifty-three requests for the first session, forty for the second, and forty for the third. Over the course of the three sessions, we would focus their thinking on reading, writing, spelling, speaking, and listening. Our goal was to get them to revisit their own learning and then look at learning as a meaning-making process. Although we discussed reading, writing, spelling, speaking, and listening separately, parents understood that we move in and out of these topics depending on the context of a situation. In planning each session we wanted to demonstrate that as advocates for children as learners we must apply the same beliefs to parents as learners. Now I would like you to step back and live some of the events that parents experienced throughout each session. The strategies and demonstrations that we used with parent/learners were the same that whole language teachers use in their classrooms.

Session #1: Reading and Writing

We opened the first session reading *Grandma's Secret* by Paulette Bourgeois. We chose this story because we felt that everyone would have a good grandma story to reflect on. This led to a discussion about the development of oral language and learning and their relationship to reading and writing. Parents indicated that, in order to facilitate spoken language, they had talked to their babies, sang or hummed nursery rhymes and songs, and read them stories. In their daily routine they had taken them out of the house to grocery stores and doctors' offices, visited friends and relatives, and continued to read to them. The environment was comfortable and allowed the children to attempt language under the watchful eyes of the parent. Parents worked on articulation, corrected grammar, and tried to develop an awareness of written language in the process. This was accomplished by using books, games, toys, magnetic letters, alphabet games, television, and the like. One parent reminds us that everyone learns when they watch children as they grow:

> Watching my children learn and grow is a most fascinating experience. My daughter (now 8 1/2) was what people call an "easy" baby. She was sociable and happy and very active. I used the term "rough and tumble" to describe her, though she was tiny. She enjoyed books early on and in my new-parent enthusiasm realized that she had a "flair" for learning. At fourteen months in fact she could walk into the middle of a set of Sesame Street flash cards and pick out the one you asked for. She would even tease me sometimes and start to reach for the wrong one with a sly smile you could detect beneath the bottle that swayed as she toddled. She had mastered this trick so well that she could even detect the card from the black and white flip side! I was so proud! And though I feel somewhat foolish looking back at what I thought was valuable to teach her, I realize now that our relationship and the fun we had doing this were far more important outcomes.

We introduced the parents to written conversation and had them try it out with another parent, pairing up and having a conversation on paper. For our purposes we asked them to find out as much as they could about their partners in five minutes. They loved this strategy!

I liked the written conversation strategy, encouraging children who may not like to write stories yet like to share (my son is one—he does not like paper and pencil tasks but I know he would find this appealing).

I thought the written conversation concept was interesting and would be helpful when working with children who may otherwise not be writing to read or converse.

I decided to have a written conversation with my husband. Between jobs and the kids it seems like we never get a chance to talk. I convinced him to try a written conversation and I was shocked at what he does at work! I had no idea what he did in any detail. Our conversation lasted about 20 minutes and I found it very revealing. I told him that we need to communicate more often on a regular basis.

Figure 5.1 shows a written conversation between a parent and her son.

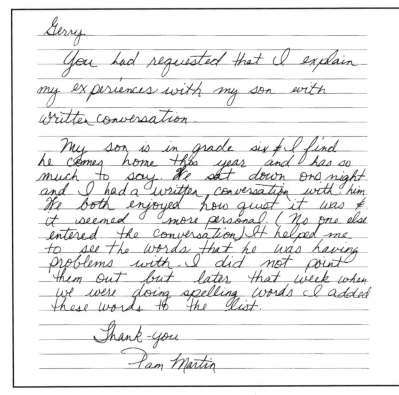

Figure 5.1. Parent/child conversation.

To introduce reading as a meaning-making event, we selected strategies from *Reading Process and Practice: From Socio-Psycholinguistics to Whole Language* (1988) by Constance Weaver. We showed them text that had letters missing from the beginnings, middles, and endings of words and asked them to read the story (see Figure 5.2).

Parents had little difficulty reading the text. They said that they could predict what the word was based on the amount of visual information presented. We discussed what goes on behind the eyes based on Frank Smith's work (1988) and the role that the eyes play in reading and in the use of visual and nonvisual print. We pointed out that the eyes really have no purpose in reading other than to pick up print from a page. Reading really is a process that takes place behind the eyes in the brain, and the main function of the brain is to search for and find meaning. The brain is capable of identifying words based on a limited amount of visual information, and in this case it only needed the first three letters of a word. In the second example (middle letters missing) parents also found it easy to read the text.

Middles absent

"W–at a mar–––ous oppo–––nity!" th–––ht L–bo. He t–ld t–e c––ld to s–op a–d p–ck fl–––rs f–r h–r gran–––ther on t–e w–y th–––gh t–e w––ds, t–en t–ok o–f on a s––rt c–t t–at o–ly t–e wo––es k–ow a––ut. S–on he ar–––ed at t–e grand–––her's co–––ge. "I–'s me, Gr–––ma," L–bo s–id in a t–ny v––ce, as he kn–––ed on t–e d–or. He pu––ed t–e d––r o–en a–d w–nt in.

Ends absent

Lob– wen– strai––– to th– grandmoth––'– be– an– gobb–––– he– up. He donn–– he– ca– an– gow– an– clim––– int– be–, feel––– non– to– wel– hims–––. By th– tim– Litt–– Re– Ridi–– Hoo– ha– arri–––, howe–––, he ha– overc––– hi– atta–– of indigest––– and wa– rea–– fo– dess–––. He answe––– Red'– kno–– in an ol–, crack–– voi––: "Com– in, dea–. Jus– com– on in."

Beginnings absent

–obo –as so –––enous –hat he ––dn't –ait –or ––ttle –ed ––ding –ood to –sk –er "–––ndma" –ow –he –as or –o ––ing –er –he ––sket of –––dies. He ––rew –ack –he ––vers, ––mped –ut of –ed, –nd –an –ver to –he ––ild. –he –––eamed –nd –an, –ut it –as –oo –ate. –obo –––bled –er up. –––erwards he –at by –he –––eside –––king –––ndma's –ipe, –––aming of ––icy ––ttle ––rls.

Figure 5.2. Text with beginnings, middles, and endings of words absent.

When we came to the third sample, parents started to struggle with the words because in this example the beginning letters were missing. At this point parents experienced a little uneasiness. We introduced them to the concepts of predicting, sampling, and confirming as strategies that support reading as a meaning-making event. The parents' difficulty also confirmed Smith's premise that the beginnings of words make it more predictable for reading, and that we only read the first three letters and move on to the next word. Most of us move back and forth through the text looking for clues to interpret or make meaning. When visual information is not sufficient or when we are not familiar with the text, we tend to miscue on certain words. We then showed them the next piece of text with the vowels missing and asked them to read it (see Figure 5.3).

Parents found they could read the text without difficulty, saying they recognized the opening as a fairy tale that began with "once upon a time," and this helped them interpret and predict the text. We seized the moment to explain to them why young children use consonants exclusively when they start to write. Since the majority of consonants have a direct one-to–one sound-to-letter correspondence, spelling by consonants is easier. It also allows young writers an opportunity to communicate their message and has tremendous implications for language development. When students start to incorporate vowels into their writing, we see variations of their use because vowels are not as predictable as consonants, often performing many sound functions

---

Vowels absent

-nc- -p-n - t-m- th-r- w-s - h-nds-m- y--ng w-lf
n-m-d L-b-. L-b- l-v-d w-th h-s m-th-r -nd f-th-r
-t th- -dg- -f - d--p, d-rk w--ds. -v-r d-- L-b-
w-nt t- h-nt -t th- n-rth -dg- -f th- w--ds, n--r
th- l-ttl- v-ll-g- -f C-l--s.

Consonants absent

-o-e-i-e- a-- -o-o -ou-- -i-- -a- a -i-e-e- o--
-a--e- o- -i- -i-e, -o--i-- i- --e -ie--s -ea- --e
-oo-- o- -i--i-- -e--ie- i- --e --i--e-. A- o--e-
-i-e-, -o-o -i--- -e -u--y e-ou-- -o -i-- a --u--,
-ui-y --i-- --a- -a- -i-o-eye- i-- -a-e--- a-- ---aye-
-oo -a- --o- -o-e.

Figure 5.3. Text with vowels and consonants absent.

alone or in combination with other vowels. To illustrate the unpredict-ability of vowels, we showed the group a piece of text which had the consonants missing (Figure 5.3) and asked them to read the story. Needless to say, we made our point and made a strong connection for parents to writing and the value of invented spelling. We talked about environmental print (that is, language found in advertisements in newspapers and on road signs) and how advertising signs are used to convey messages to would-be consumers. Businesses use consonants because they can get more information on the sign, and it makes it easy for the consumer driving by to read the sign and interpret the message quickly (see Figure 5.4).

We ended by showing two pieces of text, one with the bottom part of the letters missing and one with the tops missing (Figure 5.5), and asked parents which one they found easier to read. The characters with the bottoms missing was the unanimous choice. Weaver states that this occurs because the number of letters that extend above the line of the alphabet is greater than the number of letters that extend below the line. The letters with bottoms missing allow the brain access to more visual data to predict and interpret the text.

We wanted to introduce the parents to the idea of the systems of language but did not want to use the terminology of semantics, syntax,

Figure 5.4. Environmental print sample.

and graphophonemics. We presented the parents with two types of text to read. The first piece, taken from Constance Weaver (1994), we titled, "The Corandic" (see Figure 5.6).

Uneasiness was felt in the room as parents laughed and joked about the text and shared answers to the questions. We took up the questions and asked the parents to tell us what they were thinking as they read. What strategies were they trying to use as they read the story and tried to answer the questions? They stated that they tried to

- unscramble the letters
- look for patterns (words and sentences)
- look for verbs
- identify nouns
- identify phrases that might make sense
- sound out

One of the more interesting answers was from the parent who said once she realized that she could not make sense out of the story, she

---

Bottoms absent

One day as Lobo was skirting the edge of the forest he came upon a little girl in a red hood. Her cheeks were so rosy and her arms so pudgy that Lobo knew she would be delicious. "Where are you going little girl?" he asked. "Oh," she replied. "I'm taking this basket of goodies to my grandmother on the other side of the woods. Grandma isn't feeling very well."

Tops absent

Lobo thought for a moment. He could hardly wait to devour this scrumptious child, but then again he was hungry enough to eat the grandmother too. "Which house does your grandmother live in?" asked the wolf. "In the house by the three big oak trees," said Red Riding Hood (for that is what she was called). "She lives there all by herself."

Figure 5.5. Text with bottoms and tops of letters absent.

looked at the answers and then tried to match the text in the answer to the text in the story. The fact that many parents were able to answer all four of the questions brought about a discussion regarding comprehension. Getting a perfect score on these questions had little to do with comprehending the story. We explained that students do the same thing on standardized tests. They discover very quickly how to "crack the code" and become very good at it. We explained to the parents that what they were doing cognitively was trying to access their meaning system (semantics), and when this failed they moved to alternative systems that support meaning. These included their word order system (syntax) and their sound/letter system (graphophonemics). To illustrate how we use these systems when we read, and to show that reading was a meaning-making process, we showed them another piece of text (see Figure 5.7).

Following the reading parents were asked to identify what the text was about. Most of them identified the context as "doing laundry." We asked them to share with us what strategies they used while reading the text. Most of them said that all of the systems were at work. They did not struggle with word order, sounds/letters, or meaning. It was more a question of trying to interpret the context.

Corandic is an emurient grof with many fribs; it granks from corite, an olg which cargs like lange. Corite grinkles several other tarances, which garkers excarp by glarcking the corite and starping it in tranker-clarped storbs. The tarances starp a chark which is exasperated with worters, branking a slorp. This slorp is garped through several corusces, finally frasting a pragety, blickant crankle: coranda. Coranda is a cargurt, grinkling corandic and borigen. The corandic is nacerated from the borigen by means of loracity. Thus garkers finally thrap a glick, bracht, glupous, grapant, corandic, which granks in many sarps.

a. What is a corandic?
b. What does corandic grank from?
c. How do garkers excarp the tarances from the corite?
d. What does the slorp finally frast?

Figure 5.6. Reading sample #1: The Corandic

Reflecting on Session #1

We felt excited about the morning. Before leaving this session we asked parents to reflect on the morning using "three pluses and a wish." It was obvious from their reactions that the morning session had an effect on their thinking and learning:

- I learned a great deal about how we read and found this information very enlightening.
- How individuals look at written words in a text (Lobo example).
- I had never thought about how we use consonants not vowels to put a word together.
- The clues, predict, sample, confirm.
- The process of reading—especially enjoyed "missing" letter examples.
- The link between listening, speech, and reading.
- How important it is to read to children at the age of 1–5. Never stop.
- Language—how it develops from birth. We have to learn to tune in to a child's language and learn to respond to a child's message.

The procedure is quite simple. First you arrange things into different groups. Of course one pile may not be sufficient depending on how much there is to do. If you have to go somewhere else due to lack of facilities that is the next step, otherwise you are pretty well set. It is important not to overdo things. That is, it is better to do too few things at once than too many. In the short time this may not seem important but complications can easily arise. A mistake can be expensive as well. At first the whole procedure will seem complicated. Soon however, it will become just another facet of life. It is difficult to foresee any end to the necessity for this task in the immediate future, but then one can never tell. After the procedure is completed one arranges the materials into different groups again. Then they can be put into their appropriate places. Eventually they will be used once more and the whole cycle will then have to be repeated. However, that is part of life!

Figure 5.7. Reading sample #2.

- Reading was a meaning-making event.
- I've learned that reading is not just picking up a book.
- Learned the visual effects of written words and how it's easier to understand with consonants and vowels missing (Interesting).

The above samples are representative reflections selected from approximately 250 that parents submitted. We decided to organize the second session based on the information we read from the pluses and wishes. By capitalizing on their interests, we were in a better position to meet their needs. Following the leads and capitalizing on learner interest addresses the emotional aspect of learning, which in turn makes learning enjoyable and increases the chances for the retention of information. As one parent said, "I have found several things very helpful. I like the positives stressed. I only wish that the course had been a little longer. I look forward to another session."

It was obvious from the comments and reflections that they wanted more strategies to use with their own children at home as well as with the students they were assigned to work with at school. Even though parents spent two-and-a-half hours during this first session, it is interesting to observe that in the comment above this parent wished the session would have been longer. Time has no boundaries when learners are engaged to the point that they are not bored or do not feel pressured to learn. The above statement, like so many others we received, supports the information in Chapter 3 and confirms our beliefs that stress-free environments make learning easy and fun.

Session #2: Reading Strategies

We began the second session reading Jon Scieszka's *The True Story of the 3 Little Pigs* and Sheryl McFarlane's *Waiting for the Whales*. We discussed how to know a good book and suggested using the following as a guide:

How to Know a Good Book
- Richness of the language
- Uniqueness in style, illustration, or text
- Story invites a response
- Appealing format
- Enduring quality

The following is a description of how we used four strategies with the parents to address reading as a process of constructing meaning using predicting, sampling, and confirming text. The four strategies were:

1. Directed Reading-Teaching Assignment
2. Say Something
3. Bookmarks
4. Miscue Analysis

Directed Reading-Teaching Assignment

To demonstrate reading as a meaning-making process we began with a directed reading-teaching approach (DRTA) using the story *Very Last First Time* by Jan Andrews and Ian Wallace (1986). The purpose of a DRTA is to get the audience to predict what they think the text might be about, read or listen to the text read, and confirm or reject their original predictions and generate new predictions based on the new information. By making predictions and sampling the text to confirm or reject their predictions, parents were coming to view reading as a process of constructing meaning. Averil started by reading the title and asking the parents to predict what they thought the story might be about. When Averil paused during the reading, I recorded the parents' predictions on an overhead transparency (see Figure 5.8).

Whenever Averil paused, the group would look at the predictions and decide if they could confirm any of the predictions. If they could, we drew a line from the prediction side of the page to the confirmed side. If there was something that the group felt was not relevant at all, a line was drawn through it. By the end of the story only accurate predictions remained. What occurs during a DRTA is discussion, negotiating of the predictions, and excitement over confirmations. Parents had the following reactions:

> The idea of predicting what will come next in a story seems to be an excellent way of getting a child involved and participating.
>
> I like having the names for the parts of the process--predicting, sampling, confirming. Reading is so much a part of us we sometimes find it hard to analyze it into chunks others can handle.
>
> Confirming and predicting. I don't recall predicting or asking the children to predict so that was new to me.

Say Something

We selected this strategy from *Creating Classrooms for Authors* (Harste, Short, & Burke, 1988). In this strategy parents were paired up and given copies of the same novel. They were asked to decide between them who would begin reading, and that person would read a paragraph silently and then say something about what they read to the partner. The partner, who also would have read the paragraph, would listen, and when the first reader was done talking the partner would

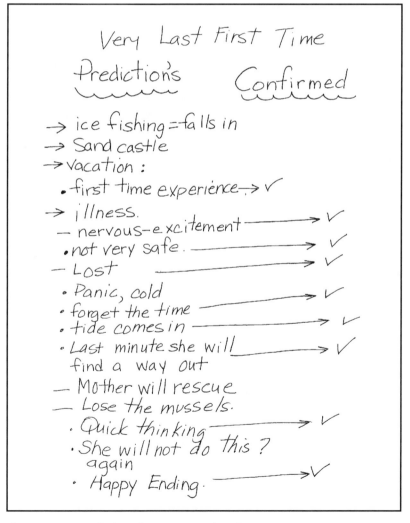

Figure 5.8. Predictions for *Very Last First Time.*

read the next paragraph and say something about the text to the first reader. Parents were asked to read a page or two using the strategy of "saying something" to their partners about the text. Following the activity we discussed their reactions to reading and responding to the text. Parents felt that they had to follow along as their partners read so that they would be able to say something when their turn came. They found that saying something led to discussing other features or opinions about the story. Some of the parents commented that they found themselves starting to predict to one another what might happen next in the story.

Discussing each paragraph after reading it will certainly increase the reader's comprehension skills.

Reading silently a paragraph at a time and asking questions was such an interesting idea.

Say Something was useful in testing understanding of a story.

Say Something as an oral experience was a nice lead-in to Bookmarks as a strategy.

Bookmarks

Bookmarks is a strategy that Linda Crafton (1991) describes in her book *Whole Language: Getting Started . . . Moving Forward*. Parents used the same books for this strategy as for Say Something and were provided with slips of paper cut to the same size as a standard bookmark. The purpose of this strategy was to have them read a page and copy down one or two things they thought were the main points. They were told that since this was not going to be published they were not to worry about spelling, punctuation, and grammar. They were asked to copy down the page number on each bookmark in case the bookmarks were lost. Parents read three pages and completed a bookmark for each page. During our discussion of this strategy, parents felt that there were many variations and extensions that could be done with this strategy. They thought that once students finished reading a chapter they could take their bookmarks and share them with other students and find out how similar or different they were to one another. The parents felt that this would open up a forum for literature discussion. Once the students read the entire book they could remove all of their bookmarks and use them to write a book review. The point form statements on the bookmarks would be the highlights or key features of each chapter and therefore would provide the framework for writing.

Miscue Analysis

The questions dealing with oral reading concerned many parents. Many of them wanted to know what to do with children who substitute or omit words when they read, when to correct a word that has been mispronounced, and what to do with students who read well orally but do not seem to understand a story. We started by referring parents to the systems of language, reminding them that when we read for meaning it is not necessary to read or pronounce every word in order to comprehend a story. We used the example of silent reading. If there were some way that we could monitor silent reading, we would find that people leave out and substitute words on a regular basis. Also, when they read silently, people move back and forth through the text to negotiate meaning. We see this happening by observing adult readers going back to certain pages of a book to locate information about a character to keep the plot and story line in place. To help parents understand miscues and how miscues tell us what readers know about language, we used cloze passages with environmental print (see Figure 5.9). Cloze passages are sentences or paragraphs that have certain words deleted from the text. The reader uses other textual or visual clues to provide a word that would maintain the meaning of the text.

Figure 5.9. Cloze passage using environmental print.

We asked parents to provide a word for the passage. Responses showed that the words were similar in meaning, and, based on a person's previous experience with a context, the word an individual would have used to complete the passage was probably related to that experience. We related this to oral reading and what to do when children miscue on a word. We suggested that parents

- wait and allow the child time to think
- not say anything or provide any verbal clues
- encourage the child to attempt saying the word
- realize that self-correcting is good
- do a retrospective miscue analysis

Many parents said that their first reaction is to tell the child the word or to try to sound it out with the child because this was the way they were taught. The most frequently asked question was, "If a child when reading comes across a word he or she has not seen before and mispronounces it, when do you correct them?" We suggested a retrospective miscue analysis where parents keep track of the miscues during reading (by recording them by hand or using audiotape) and then sit with the child, go back through the text pointing out what the text said and what they said, and discuss the differences. Revisiting the text in this fashion provides the student with an opportunity to build on what they already know about sounds, letters, and words while at the same time giving the parents a good idea of the child's growth as a reader. The final thing we suggested to the parents to see if the student comprehended the story or text was to conduct a retelling. From the retelling the parent would be in a better position to determine if any of the omissions or substitutions support comprehension or whether the student relies on sounding out as his or her primary strategy when reading.

Reflecting on Session #2

Following our session parents felt that they had a better understanding of reading development and no longer viewed the miscues as negative.

This was very interesting. I am not as concerned as I was about printing, reading and phonics. I now have new ideas of how to help.

How lucky my own children are to be able to improve their reading and writing skills through the knowledge I have attained through this program.

I have three children in grades 2, 3, and 5. I now have a greater understanding of all.

Our final session dealt with writing and spelling, both areas where parents have many concerns and questions.

Session #3: Writing and Spelling

We took the notion of miscues into writing and focused this session on the questions parents had about spelling and writing. We examined writing samples of children from kindergarten to grade 8 and demonstrated strategies that can be used with children to develop their knowledge of words, sounds, letters, and language. To help parents understand that sounding out words as a criterion for good spelling is only one strategy that people use, we began by showing them a list of words (see Figure 5.10) taken from Bill Bryson's book *The Mother Tongue: English and How It Got That Way* (1990, p. 121). The words in the right column were covered, and parents were asked to identify how many of the words on the left they thought were spelled incorrectly. They were not allowed to work with anyone, and we insisted on quiet in the room. In doing so we created stress, and knowing (as we saw in Chapter 3) that stress causes the brain to "shut down" or look for "safe routes," the parents were forced to use alternative strategies with the list of words. You might want to try this on some of your friends or colleagues to illustrate what the parents discovered, or cover up the right side of the list right now and try it yourself.

When we asked the group to identify how many of the words were spelled incorrectly, we received a range of answers from five to ten. In actuality all fifteen words are misspelled. When we shared this fact with the parents, many of them started to challenge us on the accuracy of the words. (By the way, most of the parents missed the spelling of the word "misspelled" in the instructions at the top of the page—how did you do?) This was not an uncommon result, so we asked the parents to tell us what strategies they used to determine if the words were spelled correctly. The majority said that their first reaction was to rely on sounding out. Since we had requested that there be no talking, they could not confirm with others whether they were right or wrong. Also, there were no textual sources for them to access. There was no environmental print in the room, and they did not have access to dictionaries and thesauri to confirm or reject their answers. I explained that these restrictions isolated them on the sound/letter system of language (graphophonemics). This exercise demonstrates that when we are faced with decisions of spelling accuracy, we essentially access two strategies: how words sound and how they look. The parents first tried to use their knowledge about sounds and letters, and when they could not confirm their predictions they tried to determine if the words "looked right." Now, once they were in this position they needed to confirm or reject their responses, but since we placed restrictions on the environment they could go no further and anxiety set in. When this happened many of them said they started to feel a little frustrated. To illustrate how we shift from sounding to visual strategies, I used the example of someone wanting to write a word like *accommodate* in a letter or a note. When you come to the word and are not sure how to spell it, you will try to

---

Just as a quick test, see if you can tell which of the following words are mispelled.

supercede	supersede
conceed	concede
procede	proceed
idiosyncracy	idiosyncrasy
accomodate	accommodate
dexterious	dextrous
impressario	impresario
irresistable	irresistible
rhythym	rhythm
opthamologist	ophthalmologist
diptheria	diphtheria
anamoly	anomaly
caesarin	caesarean
grafitti	graffiti

Figure 5.10. Spelling list.

sound it out first; if this fails you move to a secondary visual strategy by going off the paper and writing options that might look like this:

accommodate
acommodate
accomodate
accommodate

At this point learners shift from sounding-out to visual strategies. With a word like *accommodate*, the problem we usually have (if we have not internalized the correct spelling) is with the number of c's and m's. By writing out the word we visually reconstruct the word and make an accurate prediction of the correct spelling. But many people get to this point and want to be certain their guess is correct, so they rely on a textual source to confirm their choice.

Children are no different. However, I have come to view children as "survivors." In the interest of survival they will manipulate two sources: humans and texts. It is only natural (and easier) to ask someone when you are not sure of the spelling of a word. When we remove this option, we limit the chances for learning the correct spelling and we force children to abandon their desires to use "rich" vocabulary and force them into relying on "safe" language when they write. That is why whole language classrooms value the social nature of learning. But we need not stop there. Had I made dictionaries and thesauri available on the tables when we first asked the parents to identify the correct spellings from the list, they would have scrambled to the dictionaries to confirm their predictions. Again, kids are no different. It is why whole language teachers create print-rich environments and encourage students to use one another as sources.

I shared with the parents a story about spelling and my grade 4 class. I had a standing rule when it came to spelling: there were thirty-two children in our class; if they didn't know how to spell a word, they could come to me only after they had asked other students (the principal, janitor, secretary, and anyone else who walked into the room were also fair game). At first the class thought this was great. As I observed some of them going around the room trying to access a human source, however, I saw that many of them gave up after five or six tries, muttering, "Well if you won't tell me then I will use the dictionary."

The parents now understood from both this strategy and the missing letters strategy that sounding out is not the only way to spell or read. The parents were ready to look at some children's writing samples to put this information in the context of writing. Our purpose was to get parents to look at what children know about language and show them how to use this information with their students. Figure 5.11 shows my son Jarrod's dinosaur story (written at the age of 6.3).

Parents identified the following aspects of Jarrod's writing:

- strings of letters
- some spacing
- spelling of backyard "bacyrd" very close to being accurate
- other words can be identified: tyrannosaurus, with, pterodactyl
- drawing to support the text

Parents could see how emergent writers like Jarrod begin to develop their writing by using what they know about language. Treating these

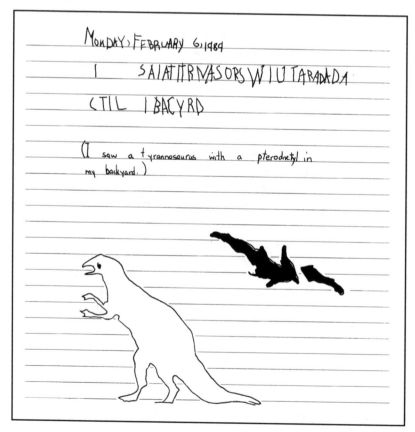

Figure 5.11. Story by Jarrod (age 6.3).

early attempts as writing and inviting the students to read them demonstrates to them how much we value their work. In the next writing sample I used a story that Jarrod wrote when he was in grade 2. We were living in South Carolina at the time, and Jarrod had gotten caught doing something to another student who was bugging him, so his teacher asked him to write a note home to his parents explaining what had happened (see Figure 5.12).

When asked to identify what Jarrod knew about language, parents pointed to

- letter format
- punctuation (commas, periods)
- abbreviations (mon.)
- contractions (I'am)
- capitalized first person pronoun (I)

With regards to his spelling, parents felt that he used sounding-out strategies (*brot/brought, rot/wrote, not/note*) and that some of his spellings had the right letters but in the wrong order (*singed/signed, middel/middle*). At this time I gave them a copy of ten of the most common strategies that students use when they spell (see Figure 5.13). I had identified these strategies in my work with fourth graders for my dissertation.

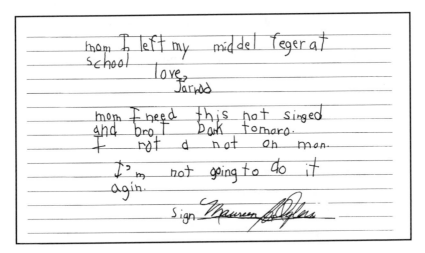

Figure 5.12. Jarrod's grade 2 writing sample.

Spelling Strategies Identified by Oglan, 1992

1. Letter name
   Each letter of the word says the name of the letter. Vowels are usually absent, e.g., first/frst, letter/ltr.

2. Spelling as it sounds
   Students rely on the sounds they hear that are close to the actual sound, e.g., uncle/uncul, feather/fethir.

3. Placeholder
   When spelling words with vowels, students will replace one vowel with another that is similar in sound, e.g., went/wont, video/vedio.

4. Representations
   Students sometimes know that a vowel is needed but insert a random vowel, e.g., misery/mazire, sometime/semtim.

5. Overgeneralization
   When students discover a new structure such as the silent e at the end of words, they use it exclusively, e.g., won/wone, from/frome.

6. Transpositional
   Words that are spelled using all of the correct letters but are in the wrong order, e.g., tried/tride, watch/wacht.

7. Visual
   The words have a visual likeness to the conventional form, e.g., school/scool, teacher/techer.

8. Articulation
   Vowels and consonants are close in sound and are usually used interchangeably, e.g., combat/kombat, graphics/grafics.

9. One letter misses
   The word is close to the conventional form with the exception of a letter, e.g., snowed/snowd, waiting/wating.

10. Multiple strategies involve combinations of strategies
    For example, neighborhood/nebrhode, retirement/ritearment

Figure 5.13. Spelling strategies.

Using these strategies as a guide, we put meaning to what Jarrod was spelling and identified the word *middel/middle* as a transpositional spelling. Transpositional spellings are words that have all of the correct letters but in the wrong order. I generally ignore transpositional strategies because they are strong signs of growth that mean that the student is on the verge of internalizing the correct spelling. The example of the word *singed/signed* here demonstrates how students move in and out of the systems of language: at the end of the story we see that where Jarrod wants his mother's signature, the word *sign* is spelled conventionally. With words like *left/lift* he used a placehold strategy where one vowel is replaced by a vowel that has a similar sound (short e and short *i*). He accessed a rhyming pattern for *rot/wrote* and *not/note*, used a sounding-out strategy on *tomoro/tomorrow* and *feger/finger*, and for the word *agin/again* there may have been a southern dialect at work.

We discussed how adults (because of the empirical paradigm) are accustomed to seeing error when we look at a child's writing. Our eyes are immediately drawn to the "mistakes," and in the process we ignore what the student knows about language. Using what I describe as a "surface-level score" brings new meaning to an urge to gravitate toward error. A surface-level score is found by adding up the number of words used in a piece, identifying the invented spellings, subtracting them from the total, and ending up with the total number of conventional words spelled correctly. To demonstrate how we gravitate to error, I showed them a journal entry from Jesse, a fourth-grade student (see Figure 5.14).

Parents read the story and felt that Jesse made a lot of mistakes. Before we looked at identifying the strategies he used and what he knew about language, we completed a surface-level score. We found that the spellings Jesse used in his story were approximately 63 percent conventional and 37 percent invented. This result surprised the parents because on the surface this ratio appeared not to be the case. From this I cautioned parents that a high rate of conventional (safe) spelling is not always a good sign. I showed them a story written by a student in grade 7 (Figure 5.15).

This story used a total of 161 words; four of the words were invented and 157 were conventional spellings. What does this tell us? This student used "safe" language. Although he filled almost one page with text, the language he used was not consistent with the language development we would expect from someone in seventh grade. Even his invented spellings demonstrate that he is not a risk taker in his writing: *cloths* for *clothes* and *unconsious* for *unconscious*. As parents we cannot judge a story by its length; however, this seems to be a very common practice in schools as a criterion for evaluating writing.

Reflecting on Parents as Learners

These experiences demonstrate the paradigm issue discussed in Chapters 1 and 2. Parents cannot be expected to make a shift without support from the teacher and the school. Following this session parents felt they were in a much better position to help the students they work with as well as better understand their own children's writing and spelling.

> Thank you! I have found several things very helpful. I like the positives stressed. I only wish that the course had been a little longer. I look forward to another session.

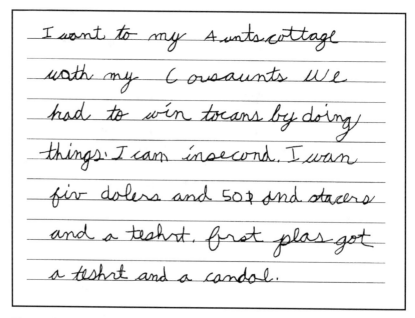

Figure 5.14. Jesse's story.

I have learned a lot from this program and I will try to use the strategies in the school.

This was great! The program gave me a "more" open mind. The reading, word play, and writing strategies were of benefit.

This was a wonderful experience. I hope that teachers are regularly exposed to this sort of information too!

I feel uplifted and feel like I can really help children in our schools.

I now have new insights on how children learn to spell and read. Some of the material I have tried with success with my son.

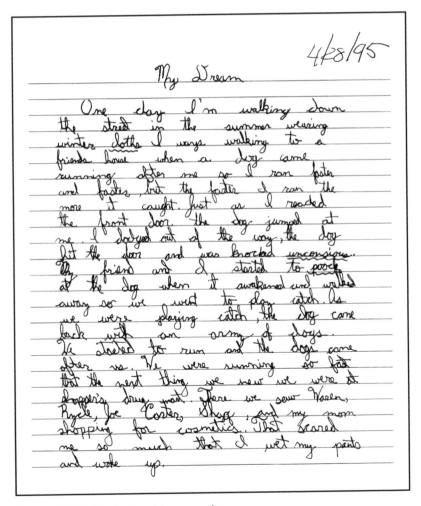

Figure 5.15. Grade 7 writing sample.

I am not as concerned as I was about printing, reading, and phonics. I have ideas of how to help out.

I thank you for creating in me a parent who is excited to be a volunteer in my school. I will keep your insights with me always and share with others all that I have learned! Three cheers for recognizing how valuable our children really are!

I felt extremely overwhelmed at the end of these three short days. I have learned more about my child's potential knowledge and I am anticipating being able to incorporate it. I thank you for making sense of my son's reading program.

I'm intrigued to learn more. I would do this program again every week if able. I will try to adopt the techniques learned.

Over the course of these three sessions, the groups of parents became a community of learners. They asked if they could continue meeting, they wanted to visit each other's schools, and most of all, they wanted more sessions so they could continue learning.

6 Educational Reform: Pendulum Swing or Paradigm Shift?

School communities have the responsibility to develop an atmosphere in which diverse perspectives on learning are valued and engaged in dialogue as part of decision making.

—IRA/NCTE Joint Task Force on Assessment, 1994.

The standards movement across North America devotes a great deal of attention to "community." I would like to share with you excerpts from the *Report of the Royal Commission on Learning,* published by the Ontario Ministry of Education in 1994, the IRA/NCTE *Standards for the Assessment of Reading and Writing,* also published in 1994, and the NCTE/IRA *Standards for the English Language Arts,* published in 1996. By highlighting similarities between the reports with regards to community and parents, we can recognize the implications this information has for classroom teachers and for the role that parents can play in the education of their children. Based on this information the role of parents in our schools must change from more traditional roles as volunteers to a view of parents as learners.

The Royal Commission Report

*F*or the Love of Learning: Report of the Royal Commission on Learning was the result of a twenty-month study conducted by a six-member committee established by the Ontario government in 1993. The committee traveled across the province visiting twenty-seven cities, holding public hearings for anyone or any group who wanted to have their say in restructuring education in Ontario to meet the needs of learners and society as we move into the twenty-first century. The committee heard from parents, teachers, students, trustees, school administrators, the business community, francophone groups, multicultural organizations, aboriginal groups, unions, colleges, universities, librarians, social workers, police officers, doctors, and members of religious groups. They visited schools regularly and held news conferences that were taped and aired by cable and television networks on a regular basis. By the time they had completed their visitations and public forums, the committee had received more than 1,500 written submissions as well as video- and audiocassettes. The data represented the feelings, views, and opinions of Ontario's diverse culture.

Standards for the English Language Arts

*T*he project was initiated in 1991 when a letter was sent to the U.S. Secretary of Education from Judith Thelen, then president of the International Reading Association (IRA) and Shirley Haley-James, then president of the National Council of Teachers of English (NCTE). The letter stated that if the federal government were to fund a voluntary standards project in English, IRA and NCTE wanted to be involved.

In the fall of 1992 the U.S. Department of Education awarded a grant for the Standards Project for the English Language Arts. Educators at the Center for the Study of Reading at the University of Illinois would work closely with IRA and NCTE to develop the standards. Federal involvement ended in 1994, and from that time the project was funded solely by IRA and NCTE. Thousands of K–12 teachers were involved in all aspects of creating, editing, and revising the document. Hundreds of parents, legislative leaders, administrators, researchers, and policy analysts played a critical role at each phase of the project.

The Reports and Language Learning

Both documents imply that learning is a generative process that takes place over the course of a lifetime. No one ever "arrives," so to speak, at a point in his or her life where learning stops. On the contrary, both documents support the belief that learning is in a constant state of flux and is not limited to any age. Both documents framed this idea with a set of standards or learning outcomes that students are expected to achieve (see Figures 6.1 and 6.2).

1. All language skills—listening, speaking, reading, writing, viewing, and representing—are equally important. They are interconnected, and the student's progress in one area influences and is influenced by developing in other areas.

2. Students are most likely to develop language competence, as well as thinking and social skills, when they have opportunities to use language to communicate for real purposes and in real situations, both in the academic context of the classroom and in the broader community.

3. Students are more likely to learn appropriate and correct language use in speech and in writing through extensive practice in reading and writing than through the use of rules in isolation. The study of the uses and conventions of language, including those relating to grammar, spelling, and punctuation, should increase gradually as students develop their language skills.

4. All students pass through the same stages in developing their language skills, but may differ in their pace and ways of learning. A certain minimum fluency is required before students are able to reflect critically on their own language use.

5. Language, culture, and identity are closely linked. A program that recognizes, respects, and values students' racial, cultural, and linguistic backgrounds, as well as varieties of language, helps them develop a positive sense of self and motivates them to learn. All students need opportunities to think critically about the social values and status assigned to different languages by various groups in our society and to explore issues of bias and stereotyping related to language and culture.

6. First-language literacy is important for second-language learning. It helps students to grasp key concepts more easily and influences general academic achievement.

7. Knowledge of a second language strengthens first-language skills. It also helps students to understand the value of other languages and cultures.

Figure 6.1. Language Standards—Ontario.

1. Students read a wide range of print and nonprint texts to build an understanding of texts, of themselves, and of the cultures of the United States and the world; to acquire new information; to respond to the needs and demands of society and the workplace; and for personal fulfillment. Among these texts are fiction and nonfiction, classic and contemporary works.

2. Students read a wide range of literatures from many periods in many genres to build an understanding of the many dimensions (e.g., philosophical, ethical, aesthetic) of human experience.

3. Students apply a wide range of strategies to comprehend, interpret, evaluate, and appreciate texts. They draw on their prior experience, their interactions with other readers and writers, their knowledge of word meaning and of other texts, their word identification strategies, and their understanding of textual features (e.g., sound-letter correspondence, sentence structure, context, graphics).

4. Students adjust their use of spoken, written, and visual language (e.g., conventions, style, vocabulary) to communicate effectively with a variety of audiences and for different purposes.

5. Students employ a wide range of strategies as they write and use different writing process elements appropriately to communicate with different audiences for a variety of purposes.

6. Students apply knowledge of language structure, language conventions (e.g., spelling and punctuation), media techniques, figurative language, and genre to create, critique, and discuss print and nonprint texts.

7. Students conduct research on issues and interests by generating ideas and questions, and by posing problems. They gather, evaluate, and synthesize data from a variety of sources (e.g., print and nonprint texts, artifacts, people) to communicate their discoveries in ways that suit their purpose and audience.

8. Students use a variety of technological and informational resources (e.g., libraries, databases, computer networks, video) to gather and synthesize information and to create and communicate knowledge.

9. Students develop an understanding of and respect for diversity in language use, patterns, and dialects across cultures, ethnic groups, geographic regions, and social roles.

10. Students whose first language is not English make use of their first language to develop competency in the English language arts and to develop understanding of content across the curriculum.

11. Students participate as knowledgeable, reflective, creative, and critical members of a variety of literacy communities.

12. Students use spoken, written, and visual language to accomplish their own purposes (e.g., for learning, enjoyment, persuasion, and the exchange of information).

Figure 6.2. NCTE/IRA Standards.

Both documents support a pedagogical paradigm shift from skills in isolation to incorporating a global perspective that recognizes gender and racial equity and cultural issues. Someone reading between the lines and envisioning what classrooms based on these standards might look like would see classrooms far different from the ones in which our students' parents were educated. Many teachers might also fear that these classrooms are different from the ones in which they have been teaching. As discussed in Chapter 3, when the human brain is confronted with fear, it seeks safe havens to deal with the fear. For some teachers the standards could spell d-i-s-a-s-t-e-r and could have some of them asking questions like the following:

- Who will be responsible if a student does not achieve a standard?
- Will parents say it is the responsibility of the teacher?
- Will the teacher say it is a student problem?

School districts and boards of education have been given the responsibility to incorporate the standards and outcomes into their curricula. In the province of Ontario, school boards are attempting to do this by taking each standard/outcome and breaking it down into isolated skills at each grade level. The resulting curriculum documents are given to teachers in large three-ring binders. There is a binder for language arts and one for mathematics, with subjects like history and geography to follow. Some teachers are overwhelmed by these documents. Time, money, and energy will be spent on professional development to explain these documents, and many teachers will take them back to their classrooms and, feeling frustrated due to a lack of direction, will place them on a shelf and go on teaching what they feel students need, complaining about the "old pendulum swing again." As one veteran teacher said following a professional development session, "Nothing new, same thing, just worded differently." Is this really what we want teachers to think? If so, then these documents and the standards and outcomes movement will have failed to create a new paradigm for learning.

The Reports and Parental Involvement

The documents, as well as the *Standards for the Assessment of Reading and Writing*, place a strong emphasis on parental involvement far different from the traditional notion. The documents suggest that parents be part of inservice and professional development programs alongside teachers and administrators. Are teachers ready for this? Are parents who work in schools as volunteers willing to devote time to inservice? Consider the following excerpts from both of the documents on parents. First, the Royal Commission on Learning:

> Just as the research is clear about the positive impact of involving teachers in school management, so it's equally strong about the positive role parents can play in their kid's education. Nothing motivates a child more than a home where learning is valued. If parents show a close interest in their children's school progress, help with homework and home projects, and attend their kids' various school performances and sports events, their kids are more likely to have higher student achievement, higher aspirations, better atten-dance, and a more positive relationship with their teachers. That's why for us, this form of parental involvement takes precedence over all others, and we've described it as a priority for every principal and teacher to take active steps to help parents do exactly those things. (p. 49)

Second, the IRA/NCTE *Standards for the Assessment of Reading and Writing* state as follows:

> The responsibility for parental involvement lies on both parents and schools. Parents must seek ways to become involved, and schools must organize to include parents in their assessment and staff development programs, and actively seek their participation. . . . Involving parents in the assessment process includes involving them in staff development or community learning projects in which they learn more about reading and writing. It also includes the use of communication and reporting procedures between school and home that enable parents to talk in productive ways with their children about their reading and writing. Involving parents and parent committees in the development of new reporting procedures is essential, since they are the primary audience for such reports. (p. 38)

It will take a concerted effort by a number of groups to come to a consensus on what professional development programs might look like for parents and how, when, and where these programs might be implemented. Can teachers accept the fact that they might be sitting next to a parent at their next inservice? I believe that it is possible to have such a system if all of the key figures (or in this case adults) see themselves as learners in the process and move toward an interpretive and collaborative model. In such a case, everyone must come back to the zero point on the number line (mentioned in Chapter 2 on paradigms) and begin to construct this new paradigm together.

What about Whole Language?

For the last decade whole language has been a moving force in questioning existing beliefs about learning to read and write. In doing so the whole language movement has compiled a substantial research base that identifies what it took the Royal Commission and NCTE/IRA to realize in terms of time, money, and human investment. No, it is not standards or outcomes, but rather what is behind the message and what whole language teachers know and believe about learning:

- learning is a social phenomenon
- teachers respect the knowledge all learners bring into the classroom or any learning event
- learning is multimodal
- teachers view themselves as learners
- language learning is embedded in and across all subjects
- ownership and responsibility for learning is student centered
- students, teachers, and parents have a voice in the education of children

The parents and teachers I work with seem to think that whole language is on its way out, soon to be replaced by outcomes and standards. I suspect the opposite to be true. Given what the standards say about diversity, community, assessment, and curriculum, the educational community should revisit whole language research to examine the power and potential it has had in its beliefs about literacy. Then maybe educators will stop shifting the accountability when the standard is not reached and instead adopt more of an interpretive understanding of learning. We should not limit our comments to educators; parents have to be included. In doing so it will take time to demonstrate to parents whole language theory and philosophy. The suggestions and examples that I used in Chapter 5 can be a start. But don't look to them as an opportunity to pacify an angry parent; rather, view them as an opportunity to initiate conversation and discussion about learning as a meaning-making event. Having parents recall their own education histories can be a wonderful way to emphasize the issue of emotion and learning. The easy/hard activity in Chapter 3 seems simplistic, but it supports what Kenneth Goodman says about language learning and it demonstrates patterns between parent learners. The fact that some parents found spelling easy to learn while others found it hard should be discussed, but I could almost bet that you will find it wasn't the speller, weekly tests, or the number of stickers on the spelling chart that made the difference. However, through your discussion you might find that a special teacher, a friendly room, a close friend, or a parent or another adult was the crucial factor.

Some Final Thoughts on Parents

Parents make sense of a test score or a report card grade or comment based on their own schooling history, beliefs, and values.

—NCTE /IRA Joint Task Force on Assessment, p.11.

I asked parents what they wanted their children to get out of their experiences at school. The following represent some of the answers I received:

- a joyful learning experience
- appreciation of learning
- interest in learning
- a good grasp of the basics, e.g., elements of math, sentences and grammar, exposure to the spelling of words
- respect for each other
- organizational skills
- freedom to create and express on their own
- responsibility in a "community" surrounding

How will these wishes be dealt with in the face of educational reform? As the standards movement in North America becomes more and more a reality, what impact will this have on curriculum, instruction, teaching materials, teacher education, professional development, assessment, and evaluation? What role will parents play in the process of educational restructuring? Must we wait and wonder who will answer these questions? Now is the time for communities to come together, to join forces in the interest of our children, and to initiate conversation. Through conversation everyone's voice will be heard and action will be the result of a negotiated approach to literacy. The "parent dilemma" then becomes "our dilemma" in which educators must demonstrate for parents what a whole language curriculum looks, sounds, and feels like.

While I was attending a practice of my son's hockey team, a parent commented to me, "You are a teacher, you must get tired of all of the teacher bashing going on." He went on to explain that he had recently received his property tax bill and had calculated that it costs approximately fifteen dollars to send his two children to school for a day. "Where can I send my children for fifteen dollars a day where they will get the attention they do from trained adults, be challenged, learn a variety of things, and most of all, be safe and for the most part happy?" He has a point! We joked how the public is quick to jump all over education, yet some parents will not hesitate to send their children to day camps in the summer at a cost of sixty to seventy-five dollars a day (four to five times what they pay to send their children to school each day). What accounts for their willingness to spend so much more on camp? Is it because parents choose to send their children to a camp? Is it because they have read materials or discussed the program with the camp officials? Is it because their children have expressed an interest in wanting to go to camp? Parents are willing to "invest" money and time in the better interest of their children when their concerns and questions are answered. As a result they feel comfortable knowing that their children are happy and safe. Can the same be said about school? Shouldn't the experiences and memories of our education be as pleasant as our memories of camp? In order to make this happen the camp directors (teachers, administrators, trustees, parents) need to view one another as collaborators with the task of making their community camps (schools and classrooms) pleasant experiences.

The questions posed by parents in this book reveal a dilemma about parental concern over what is being taught and how. Take an issue like invented spelling. Where in North America can you go where this issue hasn't been debated ad nauseam? The media jumped all over it, researchers attempted to explain it, and parents wanted to talk about it. That's when the real problems began. Educators who lacked the ability to articulate to the public what they knew about invented spelling and why they allowed it retreated to "safe havens." The safe havens shifted responsibility and ownership of curricular decisions away from the individual teacher and threw it onto the shoulders of the principal, consultants, or school district supervisors. The questions posed in this book demonstrate that teacher beliefs drive the classroom curriculum and will continue to do so even in the face of the standards movement. Without standards parents were beginning to make observations about teachers. "Why did my son write so well in Mrs. Smith's room last year and this year he hates writing?" The parents I worked with over three years expressed concern that a lot of the information they received through the workshops was not evident in their children's classroom. One reason is that the majority of whole language teachers on any given staff are outnumbered by traditional staff members. The parents of a child in a whole language classroom soon discover anomalies like the one mentioned above. They often ask, "I really like this program, but what will happen when my child moves to the next grade and has one of the more traditional teachers who value a skill-and-drill approach?" This is one of the hardest questions a whole language teacher faces because it is loaded with ethical, philosophical, and political ramifications. Whole language teachers are caught between what they know about learning and the limitations of their colleagues who emerge as critics against anything that challenges or threatens their programs. Traditional teachers play on the educational experiences of parents by showing them how their programs focus on spelling, grammar, and skills that were lacking in the whole language classroom. To change this situation, whole language teachers must become proactive. They need to demonstrate what they know about learning with parents and let parents experience learning through the strategies that are used with their children. At a time when teachers' schedules demand so much of their time, the very mention of an evening workshop is difficult to imagine. However, whole language teachers who invest two or three sessions with parents throughout the year find the benefits rewarding. Communicating with the home through newsletters and notes enhances the time spent with parents because the notes come back with supportive comments from parents who now have a frame of reference to rely on.

Some Final Thoughts on Teachers

Teachers seem to be easy targets. I think too much time is spent on what teachers do not do or on what they should be doing rather than on what they *have* done. We all have memories of at least one teacher who made a difference or influenced our lives in some way. These are the visions we must hold on to. I would like to share with you what the Royal Commission's report said about teachers based on their study:

> Teachers are our heroes. We believe they should be everyone's heroes. Anyone who has watched a teacher begin a day facing a group of kids who would rather be anywhere than sitting in that classroom learning about something called geometry that they could care less about understands only too well what a frustrating, thankless, enervating task these mortal women and men face so much of their working lives. In return, they feel unappreciated, disrespected, the focus of twisted media attacks, caught in an almost war-like situation not of their making. It's hardly an accident that so many teachers love talking about themselves as the front-line troops of the educational system, the ones that are in the trenches every day. Is this a happy metaphor for schooling? (p. 13)
>
> They are still out there, the naturals, the born teachers, accomplishing miracles. We've seen Grade 2 kids writing real essays and happily learning about correct spelling, grammar, and syntax in the process. We know of seven- and eight-year-olds who, under the guidance of a remarkable teacher, are having the time of their lives performing adaptations of Shakespeare, and gaining a lifelong love of the classics. We saw with our own eyes a group of teenage boys—"hormone hoppers" to their savvy teacher—so engrossed in a computer project they were doing together that they ignored the lunch bell. (p. 13)

Teachers will always hold a special place in the lives of parents, students, and the community. As this new era in education unfolds it will be marked by questioning, identifying, and rethinking many if not all of the traditional beliefs previously held about learning.

Pendulum Swing or Paradigm Shift?

I started my career in 1976 in an "open-concept" school. Open-concept schools saw the walls of classrooms removed, team teaching, and a curriculum that supported activity-based learning through small- and large-group instruction. This new approach received mixed reactions from parents and teachers. How will children learn with so much noise and activity in the room? Will they get their work completed in groups? What will assessment look like? Questions asked then seem no different than questions asked today about standards. Will the standards drive assessment? Will the curriculum change to reflect students attaining the standards? How will we assess whether students achieve a standard? And the biggest, most often-asked question is, What do we do with students who do not achieve a standard? The Royal Commission's report and the NCTE/IRA standards speak to these issues. However, educators complain about the lack of direction and specificity in the standards. Today, when I walk through the schools in my district that initiated the open-concept in the '70s, I see a far different environment. Teachers have erected portable walls and barriers. Team teaching is rare, and the activity-based curricula have given way to direct instruction. Open-concept was a pendulum swing that fell short of its goal. Will the standards follow in the open concept footsteps? I see a possibility for positive change with the standards. We have to reach teachers and parents by moving beyond explanation and shift our approach to demonstration. If anything, the standards will be fuel for conversations.

This book began with a story written by a parent, and it seems only fitting that it end the same way, from a parent who was in our parents volunteer inservice program. This is Julie's story.

When I went to school, in a small rural community, there were no questions asked about how or what I was learning. We were a homogeneous community, my parents valued our education and trusted our teachers and the administration. That was their job—they were trained to educate and to discipline. I don't remember having parents or adults other than our teachers in the building, except for concerts or parties. However, my parents knew my teachers, my classmates, and their parents, and saw them in church, buying groceries, or at our town's sports events.

Now my daughters are in a school where I don't know all the teachers, or where they come from; administration is out of my reach; and I don't know their classmates, or their classmates' parents (I suspect their teachers don't either). Can I still trust the school to teach my children appropriately? How can I even understand what teachers have to deal with? Can I/should I trust them implicitly? How can I question their approach without having knowledge of theories of education, the role of administration in teachers' decisions, the complexity of characters in the classroom? How can I learn these things if I don't have English language skills, if I don't have confidence, or, most commonly, if I don't have the time? Can I just turn off my questions and send them back to school, sign permission slips for outings, and make sure they do their homework?

I think deep down that parents want answers to these questions, they want to be active in their children's education, but they don't know how to fit in. They feel like they are in the way of teachers' important job (perhaps that same important job that they didn't understand as children), they feel that they don't know the rules of the game. Many parents feel inadequate and uncomfortable in the school setting, and this is robbing our children of valuable learning opportunities.

How exciting to see a classroom as a community of learners. I see that community including teachers and other professionals, adults and children of various nationalities and beliefs, people with skills and interests to share. School is that place where we could all meet and respect what each other already knows, and build on our own knowledge. Perhaps I'm just being too optimistic, but I want to see our children, tomorrow's leaders, exposed to this kind of community!

Last year I had an idea that would give us parents an opportunity to meet with each other, and to allow our children to host this meeting. I was willing, together with some more moms that I hoped to recruit, and with the help of the teacher, to bake some cookies with a classroom of students, and then invite their moms to a Mother's Day Social. I saw several benefits for our children, and our community:

1. *Baking is a great way to make math skills meaningful.*
2. *The project demanded cooperation from participants—who will do the mixing and who would add the flour? Will our group add chocolate chips or M&Ms, and how will that decision be made?*
3. *Invitations would be written and sent, giving meaning to a writing exercise.*

4. Mothers would be brought together in a non-threatening atmosphere, an occasion to meet each other, and see their children's environment.

5. Students would be given the opportunity to act as hosts, and ambassadors for the school and for their families.

Unfortunately the teachers I mentioned this to were not anxious to follow through. Maybe they were under too many pressures to get the regular curriculum covered: some mentioned children without mothers, or with mothers unwilling to participate. Maybe I didn't articulate my idea clearly enough (the above outline was not part of my proposal), and they probably thought it would be more work for them. Following through with a project like this would be taking risks, risking time and energy, risking children's and/ or parents' hurt feelings. I have so much respect for teachers that I don't feel right being the one to ask them to take more risks, so the idea was filed away. Maybe I'll mention it again sometime.

Parents and other volunteers in the school can be risky business for the teachers and the administration. Successful programs are the result of strong support from the principal and the teachers, and of course a willingness of people outside of the school to commit time and energy. It also takes a vision of how all these players can fit into the production of our children's future success.

Julie's story represents many features discussed in this book. She mentions memories of her school days, life in a small rural community, and the closeness of an entire community where everyone had a vested interest in the education of their children. Julie struggles with letting go of the empirical paradigm of that time and adjusting to the interpretive paradigm her children are experiencing. As a parent she feels isolation and expresses the distance felt between her children's teachers and administration compared with her education. You sense on one hand her desire to be involved with her school and on the other hand her feelings of being slighted because her suggestion about baking went unaccepted. That her belief in such an activity would foster inquiry into other subjects should be applauded; she feels rejected yet gives the teachers the benefit of the doubt because of busy schedules. She has questions. As we discussed, parents have an innate desire to know, and Julie demonstrates this desire in the second paragraph. Her doubts and fears exemplify how parents react when their questions are not answered. Parents like Julie are learning that being directly involved in instructional and curricular issues will take time. Taking classes on how children learn to read and write is a wonderful experience. Parents need to understand that being excited about their own learning is one thing, moving into the classroom is another.

What we see in Julie's dilemma is her beginning to make a shift. She fondly remembers her educational experiences and realizes that her children's will be far different. However, she also knows that for her children to be successful, she must take an active role in this process. In doing so, the resistance or reluctance from members of the teaching profession must be understood as a natural reaction. Educators are reluctant about parental involvement because it has not been defined. Teachers still see boundary lines between themselves and parents. Changing and defining what roles parents will play will take place over time. How much time? That depends on each situation. Standards have indicated that parents will be involved in schools. How will directives like this be felt in schools and communities? The information presented in this book reflects a current view of parents. Understanding who they are and how they think and why is important for educators to consider as they move toward a new era in teaching and learning.

Works Cited

Allen, J. P. B., & Van Buren, P. (1971). *Chomsky: Selected readings*. New York: Oxford University Press.

Andrews, J. & Wallace, I. (1986). *Very last first time*. New York: Simon & Schuster.

Bell, T. H. (1993). Reflections one decade after *A nation at risk*. *Phi Delta Kappan, 74*, 592–604.

Bourgeois, P. (1989). *Grandma's secret*. Toronto, Ontario: Kids Can Press.

Bryson, B. (1990). *The mother tongue: English and how it got that way*. New York: Morrow.

Caine, R. N., & Caine, G. (1991). *Making connections: Teaching and the human brain*. Alexandria, VA: Association for Supervision and Curriculum Development.

Crafton, L. (1991). *Whole language: Getting started . . . moving forward*. Katonah, NY: Richard C. Owen.

Dewey, J. (1938). *Experience and education*. New York: Macmillan.

Garvin, J. P. (1987). What do parents expect from middle level schools? *Middle School Journal, 19*, 3–4.

Glasser, B., & Strauss, A. (1967). *The discovery of grounded theory: Strategies for qualitative research*. Chicago: Aldine.

Goodman, K. S. (1967). Reading: A psycholinguistic guessing game. *Journal of the Reading Specialist, 6,* 126–135.

Goodman, K. S. (1986). *What's whole in whole language?* Portsmouth, NH: Heinemann.

Goodman, Y. M. (1989). Roots of the whole language movement. *The Elementary School Journal, 90* (2), 113–127.

Hall, N. (1987). *The emergence of literacy.* Portsmouth, NH: Heinemann.

Harste, J., Short, K. G., & Burke, C. (1988). *Creating classrooms for authors: The reading-writing connection.* Portsmouth, NH: Heinemann.

Harste, J., Woodward, V., & Burke, C. (1984). *Language stories and literacy lessons.* Portsmouth, NH: Heinemann.

International Reading Association and National Council of Teachers of English. (1996). *Standards for the English language arts.* Urbana, IL: IRA/NCTE.

IRA/NCTE Joint Task Force on Assessment. (1994). *Standards for the assessment of reading and writing.* Newark, DE & Urbana, IL: IRA/NCTE.

Kroeker, T., & Henrichs, M. (1993). *Reaching adult learners with whole language strategies.* Katonah, NY: Richard C. Owens.

Lemonick, M. D. (1995, July 17). Glimpses of the mind. *Time, 146,* 34–41.

Lincoln, Y., & Guba, E. G. (1985). *Naturalistic inquiry.* Beverly Hills, CA: Sage.

Macbeth, A. (1989). *Involving parents: Effective parent-teacher relations.* Portsmouth, NH: Heinemann.

McFarlane, S. (1993). *Waiting for the whales.* New York: Putnam.

Murphy, J. (1993). What's in? What's out? American education in the nineties. *Phi Delta Kappan, 74,* 641–646.

National Council of Teachers of English & International Reading Association. (1996). *Standards for the English language arts.* Urbana, IL: NCTE/IRA.

Newman, J., & Church, S. (1990). Myths of whole language. *The Reading Teacher, 44* (1), 20–26.

Oglan, G. R. (1992). *Spelling growth: A transactive process.* Unpublished doctoral dissertation, University of South Carolina.

Ontario Ministry of Education. (1994). *For the love of learning: Report of the Royal Commission on Learning.* Toronto, Ontario: Queen's Printer for Ontario.

Peterson, R. (1992). *Life in a crowded place: Making a learning community.* Portsmouth, NH: Heinemann.

Schubert, W. H. (1986). *Curriculum, perspectives, paradigms and possibilities.* London, Ontario: Collier Macmillan.

Scieszka, Jon. (1989). *The true story of the three little pigs.* New York: Viking.

Shannon, P. (1993). Developing democratic voices. *The Reading Teacher 47* (2), 86–94.

Shepherd, G. D., & Ragan, W. B. (1982). *Modern Elementary Curriculum.* New York: Holt.

Smith, F. (1988). *Insult to intelligence.* Portsmouth, NH: Heinemann.

Smith, F. (1989). Overselling literacy. *Phi Delta Kappan, 70,* 352–359.

Spradley, J. P. (1979). *The ethnographic interview.* New York: Holt.

Stephens, D. (1990). *What matters? A primer for teaching reading.* Portsmouth, NH: Heinemann.

Sylwester, R. (1995). *A celebration of neurons: An educator's guide to the human brain.* Alexandria, VA: Association for Supervision and Curriculum Development.

Vygotsky, L. S. (1978). *Mind in society: The development of higher psychological processes.* Cambridge: Harvard University Press.

Watson, D., Burke, C., & Harste, J. C. (1989). *Whole language: Inquiring voices.* Richmond Hill, Ontario: Scholastic-Tab Canada.

Weaver, C. (1988). *Reading process and practice: From sociopsycholinguistics to whole language.* Portsmouth, NH: Heinemann.

Weaver, C. (1994). *Reading process and practice: From sociopsycholinguistics to whole language.* (2nd ed.). Portsmouth, NH: Heinemann.

Wells, G. (1985). *The meaning makers: Children learning language and using language to learn.* Portsmouth, NH: Heinemann.

Whitin, D., Mills, H., & O'Keefe, T. (1990). *Living and learning mathematics: Stories and strategies for supporting mathematical literacy.* Portsmouth, NH: Heinemann.

About the Author

G erry Oglan was born and raised in Windsor, Ontario, Canada, and has spent the last twenty years teaching for the Windsor Public Board of Education. He spent twelve of those years working with children with learning disabilities, and as a classroom teacher he taught grades 1 to 8. He also served three years as an assistant coordinator in charge of language arts programs for grades 4, 5, and 6. Four years ago he started working with parents because he was intrigued by the questions they asked about their children's education and its connection to their own educational histories. To help parents understand learning from a whole language perspective, he conducted evening sessions for parents and co-developed the Parent/Volunteer Inservice Program. He received his doctorate from the University of South Carolina in 1992 and is presently associate professor at Wayne State University in Detroit, Michigan. He lives in Tecumseh, Ontario, with his wife and two children.

This book was typeset in Shannon by Electronic Imaging.
The typeface used on the cover was Zapf Humnst DB.
The book was printed on 60-lb. Vellum by Versa Press.